Principal Emergency Response and Preparedness Requirements and Guidance

Occupational Safety and Health Administration

U.S. Department of Labor

OSHA 3122-06R
2004

Contents

Introduction

The importance of an effective workplace safety and health program cannot be overemphasized. There are many benefits from such a program, including increased productivity, improved employee morale, reduced absenteeism and illness, and reduced workers' compensation rates. Unfortunately, workplace accidents and illnesses still occur in spite of efforts to prevent them, and proper planning is necessary to effectively respond to emergencies.

Several Occupational Safety and Health Administration (OSHA) standards explicitly require employers to have emergency action plans for their workplaces. Emergency preparedness is a well-known concept in protecting workers' safety and health. To help employers, safety and health professionals, training directors, and others, the OSHA requirements for emergencies are compiled and summarized in this booklet.

This publication provides a generic, non-exhaustive overview of OSHA standards for emergencies. It is not intended to alter or determine compliance responsibilities in OSHA standards or the *Occupational Safety and Health Act of 1970*. Please review the current OSHA standards applicable to your work operations to ensure your compliance.

NOTE: The *Americans with Disabilities Act* (ADA) imposes specific obligations on employers relative to employment of individuals with disabilities. The United States Equal Employment Opportunity Commission's website provides employer resources for addressing ADA requirements in private workplaces, including "Enforcement Guidance on Reasonable Accommodations." The Job Accommodations Network publication *Emergency Evacuation Procedures for Employees with Disabilities* provides planning information and resources on emergency procedures for employees with disabilities.

Background

The U.S. Congress passed the *Superfund Amendments and Reauthorization Act* (SARA) in 1986. This legislation included the *Emergency Planning and Community Right to Know Act* (Title III), which laid the foundation for communities to prepare for and respond to emergency incidents involving hazardous substances. Title III also requires employers to assist in planning and to provide accurate information about the hazardous substances or chemicals they control.

In 1989, OSHA issued a final rule on Hazardous Waste Operations and Emergency Response (HAZWOPER) to work hand-in-hand with SARA Title III. OSHA's rule, 29 CFR 1910.120, establishes safety and health requirements for employers for the protection of employees and requires the development of an emergency response plan. This plan is to be integrated with local, state, and Federal agency plans for local community emergency preparedness.

A second "significant" emergency planning law was enacted in 1990. The *Clean Air Act Amendments* (CAAA) gave the Environmental Protection Agency (EPA) and OSHA more responsibilities for preventing major chemical emergencies. In response to this legislation, OSHA issued the Process Safety Management (PSM) of Highly Hazardous Chemicals standard

(29 CFR 1910.119) in 1992. The standard requires employers to establish a PSM program to prevent major chemical workplace emergencies and to implement an emergency action plan.

The requirements of the HAZWOPER and PSM standards are provided in this publication. In addition, the publication includes emergency action plan and fire prevention plan requirements and emergency planning and response requirements in many other OSHA standards. In order to have an effective safety and health program, it is necessary to develop and implement emergency preparedness and response requirements that are applicable to the workplace.

The 26 states that operate OSHA-approved state plan programs set and enforce standards, such as HAZWOPER and PSM, and the other emergency planning and response requirements, which are identical to or at least as effective as Federal OSHA standards. While this publication can provide useful guidance to all employers and employees, if you are in a state with an OSHA-approved state program, you should contact the state program for specific compliance requirements.

Please note that the EPA has Risk Management Program (RMP) and Community Right-to-Know regulations that address releases of dangerous chemicals. Information is available on the EPA's website at http://www.epa.gov/epaoswer/hotline/rmp.htm.

Using This Publication

To use this publication effectively, you should review the standards identified for your industrial sector(s) and determine if they apply to your workplace. Each standard listed in this publication includes a general description of the standard's scope. Once you have determined which standards apply to your workplace, review the requirements and resources identified in this publication for each applicable standard. To assist you in better understanding each standard, this publication summarizes the essential program, procedural, equipment, and training requirements in each of the standards identified. The publication also provides online resources which discuss compliance information for implementing critical requirements.

Please note that, in developing this publication, the standards most applicable to emergency response and preparedness were included. Standards that were deemed not directly or as likely to apply to emergencies were not included. Therefore, while the majority of standards that include emergency-related requirements are addressed in this document, other OSHA standards could be applicable to a particular response action.

Publication Organization

This publication is organized so that all standards for a particular industry are grouped together. The emergency-related requirements included in this publication are grouped in the following sections: I. General Industry (29 CFR 1910), II. Shipyard Employment (29 CFR 1915), III. Marine Terminals (29 CFR 1917), IV. Longshoring (29 CFR 1918), V. Construction (29 CFR 1926), and VI. Agriculture (29 CFR 1928). Please note that a single employer could be covered by standards for more than one industry. For example, an employer in a manufacturing plant is primarily covered by 29 CFR 1910 but would be covered by 29 CFR 1926 in cases where employees are performing construction work such as erecting a new building or demolishing an old structure.

Within each group of industry standards, the standards are further organized into sections. These sections outline the emergency-related requirements as follows:

- **General Requirements for Workplaces**
  These standards are generally required of all workplaces within the industry. Every employer must comply with these requirements or the parallel state plan requirements, except where specifically exempted.

- **Additional Requirements for Workplaces Referenced in Other Requirements**
  The standards listed in this section are those that are applicable to the workplace when employer compliance is required by another OSHA standard. For example, a grain handling facility employer is required by the grain handling facility standard (1910.272) to implement an emergency action plan meeting the requirements of 1910.38. [Note: No additional requirements for Shipyard Employment, Marine Terminals and Longshoring are referenced in other requirements.]

- **Additional Requirements for Specific Workplaces/Operations**
  The standards that cover specific workplaces, operations, or processes are listed in this section. It is important to note that 29 CFR 1910.5(c) provides that these specific standards shall prevail over any other general standard which might otherwise be applicable to the same condition, practice, means, method, operation, or process. The general standards do apply, however, to the extent that none of the particular standards are applicable.

- **Requirements that Support Emergency Response and Preparedness**
  In addition to the emergency requirements contained in the sections above, this section includes standards that are likely to be applicable in an emergency situation. In any chemical-related emergency, for example, the personal protective equipment requirements are likely to be applicable. Likewise, for emergencies involving injured persons, the requirements of the bloodborne pathogens standard may apply.

I. General Industry (29 CFR 1910) Requirements for Emergency Response and Preparedness

A. General Requirements for Workplaces

1. 29 CFR 1910.36 *Design and construction requirements for exit routes*

This standard establishes requirements for the proper design and construction of exit routes. Requirements cover construction materials, opening dimensions, accessibility conditions, capacity, and special considerations for exit routes that are outside of a building.

Procedural, Program, and/or Equipment Requirements	Make exit route design permanent.
	Ensure that the number of exit routes is adequate based on the number of employees, the size of the building, its occupancy, and the arrangement of the workplace.
	Separate an exit route from other workplace areas with materials that have the proper fire resistance-rating for the number of stories the route connects.
	Ensure that exit routes meet width and height requirements. The width of exit routes must be sufficient to accommodate the maximum permitted occupant load of each floor served by the exit route.
	Ensure that doors used to access exit routes have side hinges and swing in the direction of travel (depending on occupancy and hazard areas).
	Design exit routes that lead to an outside area with enough space for all occupants.
	An outdoor exit route is permitted but may have additional site-specific requirements.
Assistance Tools	Standard – 29 CFR 1910.36 *Design and construction requirements for exit routes.*
	E-Tools – *Evacuation Plans and Procedures – Design and Construction Requirements for Exit Routes.*
	Fact Sheet – *Emergency Exit Routes Fact Sheet.*
	National Fire Protection Agency (NFPA) Code – *Life Safety Code NFPA 101.*

2. 29 CFR 1910.37 *Maintenance, safeguards and operational features for exit routes*

This standard establishes requirements for exit route lighting, marking, and non-flammable material maintenance. It also sets requirements for employee alarm systems and procedures for working during construction, repair, or alteration. Maintaining exit route standards will prepare the workplace for a successful emergency evacuation.

Procedural, Program, and/or Equipment Requirements	Maintain the fire-retardant properties of paints and solutions that are used in exit routes.
	Ensure that required exit routes and fire protections are available and maintained, especially during repairs and alterations.
	Ensure that employee alarm systems are installed, operable, and in compliance with 29 CFR 1910.165 (**Note**: See Section I.A.5.).
	Direct employees through exit routes using clearly visible signs. These signs must meet the required letter height and illumination specifications.
	When openings could be mistaken for an exit, post appropriate signs stating "NOT AN EXIT."
	Arrange exit routes so that employees are not exposed to the dangers of high hazard areas.
	Exit routes must be free and unobstructed. Prevent obstructions, such as decorations, furnishings, locked doorways, and dead-ends within exit routes.
Assistance Tools	Standard – 29 CFR 1910.37 *Maintenance, safeguards, and operational features for exit routes.*
	Interpretation Letter – February 1, 1991, Mr. Sanford B. White, *Use of Self-luminous and electroluminescent exit signs.*
	E-Tools – *Evacuation Plans and Procedure-Maintenance, Safeguards, and Operational Features for Exit Routes.*
	Checklist – *Alarm System Checklist.*
	National Fire Protection Agency (NFPA) Code – *Life Safety Code NFPA 101.*

3. 29 CFR 1910.151 *Medical services and first aid*

To handle potential workplace injuries, employers must ensure that medical personnel and adequate first aid supplies are available to workers. The selection of these resources must be based on the types of hazards in the workplace.

Procedural, Program, and/or Equipment Requirements	Ensure that medical personnel are ready and available for advice and consultation on the overall employee safety and health condition in the workplace.
	Provide trained personnel and adequate first aid supplies to render first aid when a medical facility is not in near proximity to the workplace.
	Provide suitable facilities for immediate emergency use if exposure to injurious or corrosive materials is possible.
Training Requirements	Adequately train personnel expected to administer first aid.

Assistance Tools	Standard – 29 CFR 1910.151 *Medical services and first aid.*
	Interpretation Letter – April 18, 2002, Mr. John Mateus, *Clarification of 1910.151 Medical Services and First Aid.*
	Interpretation Letter – January 6, 1995, Larry M. Starr, PhD, *The review of first aid training programs.*
	Interpretation Letter – November 1, 2002, Jennifer Shishido, *Additional clarification of using ANSI Z358.1 as guidance to comply with 1910.151(c).*
	Interpretation Letter – November 19, 1992, Mr. Shawn L. O'Mara, *Response time and "in near proximity" requirements.*
	Other Standards – American National Standards Institute (ANSI) Standard Z358.1 *Emergency Eyewash and Shower Equipment.*

4.   29 CFR 1910.157 *Portable fire extinguishers*

Employees who use portable fire extinguishers can often put out small fires or control a fire until additional help arrives. Before an emergency occurs, employers must decide whether employees are authorized to use fire extinguishers or must immediately evacuate (29 CFR 1910.38). The following section applies to portable fire extinguisher placement, use, maintenance, and testing.

Procedural, Program, and/or Equipment Requirements	Select and distribute portable fire extinguishers based on the class, size, and degree of workplace fire hazards. Mount, locate, and identify the extinguishers so they are readily accessible in an emergency and will not subject employees to potential injury.
	Provide only approved portable fire extinguishers.
	Maintain fire extinguishers. Maintenance includes monthly visual inspections, hydrostatic testing, annual internal examinations, and all associated documentation.
	Ensure that the travel distance from employee to the nearest extinguisher is appropriate for the fire class.
	Exemptions may apply when employees are expected to evacuate the workplace in an emergency action plan that meets 29 CFR 1910.38 standards. This option may effectively minimize the potential for fire-related injuries but would not authorize employees to use extinguishers.
Training Requirements	If portable fire extinguishers are provided for employee use, provide an educational program at initial employment and at least annually thereafter.
	Provide education specific to any equipment employees are expected to use as part of an emergency action plan. Provide training upon initial assignment and at least annually thereafter.

Assistance Tools	Standard – 29 CFR 1910.157 *Portable fire extinguishers.*
	Interpretation Letter – June 12, 2000, Mr. Hugh Erwin, *Soda acid and inverted foam extinguishers are not approved portable firefighting equipment.*
	Referenced Standards – 29 CFR 1910.155 *Scope, application and definitions applicable to this subpart.*
	E-Tools *Evacuation Plans and Procedures – Evaluating the Workplace - Portable Fire Extinguishers.*
	National Fire Protection Agency (NFPA) Code – *Standard for Portable Fire Extinguishers NFPA 10.*

5.   29 CFR 1910.165 *Employee alarm systems*

Employee alarm systems alert employees to begin implementing emergency action. This section applies when another OSHA standard requires an alarm to notify employees of an emergency. For example, standards that specifically require or reference alarm systems include: 29 CFR 1910.37, 1910.38, 1910.66, 1910.106, 1910.120, 1910.157, 1910.160, 1910.161, 1910.162, and 1910.164.

Procedural, Program, and/or Equipment Requirements	Provide a distinctive and perceivable alarm system for emergency action or safe evacuation.
	Specific requirements may apply if the alarm system includes telephones/manual operations, the workplace has 10 or fewer employees, or alarms serve more than one purpose.
	Ensure that all equipment used for alarm systems is approved and spare components are available.
	Test alarms at the frequency required. Follow special safety requirements for testing or restoring alarms.
Training Requirements	Establish procedures and instruct employees on when and how to sound an alarm and notify emergency personnel, and what each alarm type means.
Assistance Tools	Standard – 29 CFR 1910.165 *Employee alarm systems.*
	E-Tools – *Evacuation Plans and Procedures -- Workplace Evaluation - Alarm Systems.*
	Interpretation Letter – January 23, 1991, Mr. David A. Kruger, *Employee emergency alarm systems.*

B. Additional Requirements for Workplaces Referenced in Other Requirements

1.   29 CFR 1910.38 *Emergency action plans*

To prepare for any contingency, an emergency action plan establishes procedures that prevent fatalities, injuries, and property damage. An emergency action plan is a workplace requirement when another applicable standard requires it. The following standards reference or require compliance with 1910.38: 29 CFR 1910.119, 1910.120, 1910.157, 1910.160, 1910.164, 1910.272, 1910.1047, 1910.1050, and 1910.1051.

Procedural, Program, and/or Equipment Requirements	Identify possible emergency scenarios based on the nature of the workplace and its surroundings. Prepare a written emergency action plan. The plan does not need to be written and may be communicated orally if there are 10 or fewer employees. At a minimum, the plan must include: • The fire and emergency reporting procedures; • Procedures for emergency evacuation, including the type of evacuation and exit routes; • Procedures for those who remain to operate critical operations prior to evacuation; • Procedures to account for employees after evacuation; • Procedures for employees performing rescue and medical duties; and • Names of those to contact for further information or explanation about the plan.
Training Requirements	Review the emergency action plan with each employee when the plan is developed, responsibilities shift, or the emergency procedures change. Provide training to employees who are expected to assist in the evacuation.
Assistance Tools	Standard – 29 CFR 1910.38 *Emergency Action Plan.* Directive – CPL 02-01-037 *Compliance Policy for Emergency Action Plans and Fire Prevention Plans.* E-Tools – *OSHA's Expert System – Emergency Action Plan.* E-Tools – *Evacuation Plans and Procedures – Emergency Action Plan Checklist.* E-Tools – *Evacuation Plans and Procedures – Evacuation Elements.* Fact Sheet – *Planning and Responding to Workplace Emergencies.* Fact Sheet – *Evacuating High-Rise Buildings.* Other Agency Resources – *EPA Local Emergency Planning Committee (LEPC) Database.*

2.   **29 CFR 1910.39** *Fire prevention plans*

This plan requires employers to identify flammable and combustible materials stored in the workplace and ways to control workplace fire hazards. Completing a fire prevention plan and reviewing it with employees reduces the probability that a workplace fire will ignite or spread.

A fire prevention plan is a workplace requirement when another applicable standard requires it. The following standards reference or require compliance with 1910.39: 29 CFR 1910.157, 1910.1047, 1910.1050, and 1910.1051.

Procedural, Program, and/or Equipment Requirements	Prepare a written fire prevention plan. The plan does not need to be written and may be communicated orally if there are 10 or fewer employees. Develop a plan that includes • Major fire hazards, hazardous material handling and storage procedures, ignition sources and controls, and necessary fire protection equipment; • How flammable and combustible waste material accumulations will be controlled; • Maintenance of heat-producing equipment to reduce ignition sources; • Names or job title of persons to maintain equipment to reduce ignition sources and fire potential; and • Names or job title of persons to help control fuel source hazards.
Training Requirements	Inform employees about relevant fire hazards and self-protection procedures in the fire prevention plan when they are initially assigned to a job.
Assistance Tools	Standard – 29 CFR 1910.39 *Fire Prevention Plans.* Directive – CPL 02-01-037 *Compliance Policy for Emergency Action Plans and Fire Prevention Plans.* E-Tools – *Evacuation Plans and Procedures – Fire Prevention Plan Requirements.* Other Agency Resources – National Fire Protection Agency (NFPA) Code – *Life Safety Code NFPA 101.*

C. Additional Requirements for Specific Workplaces/Operations

1.   **29 CFR 1910.66** *Powered platforms for building maintenance*

This standard covers powered platform installations permanently dedicated to interior or exterior building maintenance of a specific structure or group of structures. It includes requirements for an emergency action plan and employee emergency action plan training.

9

Procedural, Program, and/or Equipment Requirements	Develop and implement a written emergency action plan for each kind of working platform operation. At a minimum, the plan must explain: • The emergency procedures that are to be followed in the event of a power failure, equipment failure, or other emergencies that may be encountered; and • That employees inform themselves about the building emergency escape routes, procedures, and alarm systems before operating a platform. If a platform contains overhead structures that restrict emergency egress, ensure that a secondary wire rope suspension system is provided. Provide a horizontal lifeline or a direct connection anchorage, as part of a fall arrest system, for each employee on such a platform.
Training Requirements	Train all employees who operate working platforms on the emergency action plan procedures and the parts of the plan the employees must know to protect themselves in the event of an emergency. This training must be provided upon initial assignment and whenever the plan is changed.
Assistance Tools	Standard – 29 CFR 1910.66 *Powered platforms for building maintenance.*

2. 29 CFR 1910.111 *Storage and handling of anhydrous ammonia*

This standard covers the design, construction, location, installation, and operation of anhydrous ammonia systems including refrigerated ammonia storage systems. Ammonia manufacturing plants and refrigeration plants where ammonia is used solely as a refrigerant are, however, not covered.

Procedural, Program, and/or Equipment Requirements	For stationary storage installations, provide at least two suitable gas masks with ammonia canisters for either emergency response or evacuation purposes. Provide a self-contained breathing apparatus for respiratory protection in concentrated ammonia atmospheres. For refrigerated storage systems, ensure that each compressor drive has an emergency source of power unless other measures can be taken to safely vent the vapors while the refrigeration system is not operating. For refrigerated storage systems, ensure that an emergency alarm system is installed that will activate in the event that the container(s) reach the maximum allowable operating pressure. For refrigerated storage systems, ensure that an emergency alarm system and shut-off are installed in the condenser unit that will activate in the event that there is an excess discharge pressure.

Assistance Tools	Standard – 29 CFR 1910.111 *Storage and handling of anhydrous ammonia.*
	Interpretation Letter – February 7, 1998, Mr. Jesse L. McDaniel, *Respiratory Protection for Anhydrous Ammonia Storage Installations.*

3.   29 CFR 1910.119 *Process safety management (PSM) of highly hazardous chemicals*

This section focuses on preventing or minimizing consequences from a catastrophic release of toxic, reactive, flammable, or explosive chemicals. Processes are covered by this standard when they involve quantities of highly hazardous chemicals equal to or greater than those listed in 1910.119 Appendix A, they involve flammable liquid or gas quantities greater than 10,000 pounds, or they involve the manufacture of explosives or pyrotechnics. Consult 1910.119(a) for special considerations and process exemptions. Successful PSM emergency planning relies on implementing requirements from 29 CFR 1910.38 and/or 1910.120(q).

Procedural, Program, and/or Equipment Requirements	Conduct a Process Hazard Analysis (PHA) for each covered process, and update and revalidate the PHA every 5 years.
	Incorporate emergency shutdown actions and operations into the written operating procedures for each process. Include conditions that require emergency action and the qualified operator responsible for performing these procedures.
	Implement an emergency action plan for the facility as described in 29 CFR 1910.38.
	Maintain the mechanical integrity of PSM emergency systems and alarms.
	If employees are expected to handle an emergency release rather than promptly evacuate, implement an emergency response plan according to 1910.120(q). Provide proper response and personal protective equipment for emergency responders under the plan.
Training Requirements	Review facility PSM emergency shutdown and response procedures with employees.
	Provide additional training to employees who provide response actions covered by 29 CFR 1910.120(q).
	As a host employer, clearly communicate emergency action plans with contractors. Contract employers must ensure that their employees are instructed in potential fire, explosion, or toxic release hazards related to their jobs.

Assistance Tools	Standard – 29 CFR 1910.119 *Process Safety Management of Highly Hazardous Chemicals.*
	Standard Appendix – 1910.119 Appendix A – *List of Highly Hazardous Chemicals, Toxics and Reactives (Mandatory).*
	Standard Appendix – 1910.119 Appendix C – *Compliance Guidelines and Recommendations for Process Safety Management (Nonmandatory).*
	Preamble to Final Rule – Process Safety Management of Highly Hazardous Chemicals; Explosives and Blasting Agents - *III. Summary and Explanation of the Final Rule.*
	Interpretation Letter – December 7, 1995 - Mr. J.B. Evans, *OSHA's Standard Process Safety Management of Highly Hazardous Chemicals.*

4.   29 CFR 1910.120 *Hazardous waste operations and emergency response; paragraphs (b), Safety and health program, through (o), New technology programs*

This standard covers hazardous substance cleanup operations and RCRA corrective actions (29 CFR 1910.120, (a)(1)(i) through (a)(1)(iii)). Emergency planning and response are required safety and health program elements that help minimize employee exposure and injury.

Procedural, Program, and/or Equipment Requirements	If employees are to immediately evacuate in an emergency, develop an emergency action plan in accordance with 29 CFR 1910.38. If all employees are to evacuate and an emergency action plan is developed, the employer is exempted from 1910.120(l). If employees may assist in handling the emergency, then the following requirements apply.
	As a separate section of the site safety and health plan, develop a written emergency response plan. The plan must be implemented before site operations begin and should be integrated with those of other local, state, and Federal agencies.
	Identify emergency response personnel and responsibilities in the site program's organizational structure.
	Include emergency response training details in the comprehensive site work plan.
	Identify personal protective equipment (PPE) and other equipment for emergency response in the emergency response plan.
	Install alarm systems that meet requirements of 29 CFR 1910.165.
	Share site-specific emergency response procedures with contractors and sub-contractors.
	Under certain circumstances, emergency response personnel may qualify for the medical surveillance program.
Training Requirements	Train employees assigned to respond to hazardous emergencies at cleanup sites on how to respond to expected emergencies.
	Regularly rehearse and train employees as part of the overall training program for site operations.

Assistance Tools	Standard – 29 CFR 1910.120 *Hazardous waste operations and emergency response.*
	Standard Appendix – 1910.120 Appendix B *General description and discussion of the levels of protection and protective gear.*
	Publication – OSHA 3114, *Hazardous Waste Operations and Emergency Response.*
	Safety and Health Topics – *Emergency Preparedness/Response.*
	Interpretation Letter – July 28, 1989, Richard F. Boggs, PhD, *Application of OSHA's final standard for Hazardous Waste Operations and Emergency Response.*
	Interpretation Letter – May 23, 1989, Mr. Lanny E. Partain, *Criteria for inclusion of workers in a medical surveillance program and training under 1910.120.*
	Other Agency Resources – *EPA Local Emergency Planning Committee (LEPC) Database.*
	Directive - CPL 02-02-071 *Technical Enforcement and Assistance Guidelines for Hazardous Waste Site and RCRA Corrective Action Clean-up Operations.*

5.   29 CFR 1910.120, paragraph (p) *Certain operations conducted under the Resource Conservation and Recovery Act of 1976 (RCRA)*

This section covers operations at treatment, storage, and disposal facilities regulated by 40 CFR Parts 264 and 265 under RCRA. A well established emergency response program is required to prepare employees for emergency response activities at these sites.

Procedural, Program, and/or Equipment Requirements	If employees are to immediately evacuate in an emergency, develop an emergency action plan in accordance with 29 CFR 1910.38. If all employees are to evacuate and an emergency action plan is developed, the employer is exempted from 1910.120(p) emergency requirements. If employees may assist in handling the emergency then the following requirements apply.
	Include a written emergency response plan in the employer's safety and health program. Ensure that the plan is compatible with other response agency plans and reviewed periodically to ensure currency with site conditions and information.
	Provide appropriate PPE and emergency equipment to respond to potential site emergencies.
	Install alarm systems that meet requirements of 1910.165.
	Depending on exposure circumstances, emergency responders may qualify for participation in the site medical surveillance program.
Training Requirements	Before an employee is required to perform response actions, provide training to a level of competence that protects themselves and other employees.
	Regularly rehearse the emergency response plan as part of the overall training program for site operations.
	Record and maintain training certifications that show employee attendance and completion of required training.

Assistance Tools	Standard – 29 CFR 1910.120 *Hazardous waste operations and emergency response.*
	Interpretation Letter – July 28, 1989, Richard F. Boggs, Ph.D., *Application of OSHA's Final Standard for Hazardous Waste Operations and Emergency Response.*
	Other Agency Resources – *EPA Local Emergency Planning Committee (LEPC) Database.*

6.   29 CFR 1910.120, paragraph (q), *Emergency response to hazardous substance releases*

This section covers hazardous substance emergency response operations regardless of the hazard location. The standard requires an emergency response plan and employee training and competency for anticipated emergencies. An incidental release of a hazardous substance is not covered by the standard.

Procedural, Program, and/or Equipment Requirements	If employees are to immediately evacuate in an emergency, develop an emergency action plan in accordance with 1910.38(a). If all employees are to evacuate and an emergency action plan is developed, the employer is exempted from paragraph 1910.120(q) emergency requirements. If employees may assist in handling the emergency, then the following requirements apply.
	Develop and implement a written emergency response plan that includes
	• Pre-emergency planning and coordination;
	• Personnel roles, lines of authority, training, and communication;
	• Emergency recognition and prevention;
	• Safe distances and refuge;
	• Site security and control;
	• Evacuation routes and procedures;
	• Decontamination procedures;
	• Medical treatment in emergencies;
	• Procedures for emergency alerting and response;
	• Response critiques and follow-up; and
	• PPE and emergency equipment.
	Ensure that the plan is compatible with other Federal, state, and local response agency plans and reviewed periodically for changes. The site's Local Emergency Planning Committee (LEPC) may have this information.
	Establish an Incident Command System (ICS) to coordinate response actions.
	Provide chemical protective clothing for emergency responders that is appropriate for site hazards.
	Provide backup and advance first aid support personnel ready to provide assistance or rescue. Provide equipment necessary for backup and first aid support personnel and transportation for medical care.
	Some emergency responders require medical surveillance automatically, while others may qualify only under certain exposure circumstances.

Training Requirements	Provide training to employees based on their expected duties. Train responders to one of the following levels: first responder awareness, first responder operations, hazardous materials technician, hazardous materials specialist, and on scene incident commander. Provide required training to "skilled support personnel" and "specialist employees." Ensure trainers are qualified to provide training. Provide and document annual refresher training.
Assistance Tools	Standard – 29 CFR 1910.120 *Hazardous waste operations and emergency response.* Directive – CPL 02-02-059 *Inspection Procedures for the Hazardous Waste Operations and Emergency Response Standard, 29 CFR 1910.120 and 1926.65, Paragraph (q): Emergency Response to Hazardous Substance Releases.* Directive – CPL 02-02-059, Appendix E *Releases Of Hazardous Substances That Require An Emergency Response.* Other Agency Assistance Tool – *Oil Spill Field Operations Guide ICS-OS-420-1* Other Agency Resources – *EPA Local Emergency Planning Committee (LEPC) Database.*

7.   29 CFR 1910.124 *General requirements for dipping and coating operations*

This standard establishes design, ventilation, first aid, hygiene, and maintenance requirements for dipping and coating operations.

Procedural, Program, and/or Equipment Requirements	Provide an emergency shower and eyewash station close to dipping operations. If employees work with liquids that may burn, irritate, or otherwise harm their skin, provide • Physician's approval before allowing an employee with a sore, burn, or other lesion to work in a vapor area, • Proper treatment by a designated person for skin abrasions, cuts, rashes, and open sores, • Appropriate first aid supplies near dipping and coating operations, and • Periodic exams of exposed body parts for employees who work with chromic acid.
Training Requirements	Ensure that employees know appropriate first aid procedures.
Assistance Tools	Standard – 29 CFR 1910.124 *General requirements for dipping and coating operations.*

8.   29 CFR 1910.146 *Permit-required confined spaces*

This standard requires practices and procedures to protect employees working in permit-required confined spaces (PRCS). The standard requires an evaluation to determine the existence of PRCSs, the implementation of a written permit space program, and the establishment of rescue and emergency procedures.

Procedural, Program, and/or Equipment Requirements	Provide retrieval systems or methods for non-entry rescue where feasible.
	Develop and implement procedures to summon rescue and emergency services to rescue entrants.
	Implement procedures to provide emergency services to rescued employees and prevent unauthorized personnel from attempting a rescue.
	Evaluate and select a rescuer based on his or her ability to effectively respond to a rescue in a timely manner, considering the hazard(s) identified and the types of permit spaces entered. Ensure that the responder is properly equipped and proficient.
	Provide rescuers access to all permit spaces from which rescue may be necessary, so that appropriate rescue plans are developed and rescue operations practiced.
	An employer whose employees provide permit space rescue and emergency services must provide PPE to employees, at no cost to those employees.
Training Requirements	Inform the rescuer(s) of potential hazards they may confront during rescue at the site.
	An employer whose employees provide permit space rescue and emergency services must document the training of rescuers as authorized entrants. They must also be trained in the following:
	• PPE,
	• Their assigned rescue duties, and
	• Basic first aid and cardiopulmonary resuscitation (CPR). (At least one so trained employee must be available during rescues).
	Rescuers must simulate practice rescues from actual or representative permit spaces at least annually.
	Attendants must be trained in the following:
	• The hazards that may be faced during entry,
	• Behavioral effects of hazards to entrants,
	• Maintaining count and identity of entrants,
	• Remaining outside the permit space during entry until relieved,
	• Maintaining communication with entrants to monitor and alert them if evacuation is necessary,
	• Monitoring activities inside and outside the space to ensure acceptable entry conditions and ordering evacuation if necessary,
	• Summoning rescue and other services when authorized entrants need

Training Requirements (Continued)	assistance to escape from hazards, • Taking appropriate action when unauthorized persons approach or enter a permit space, • Performing non-entry rescue according to the employer's rescue procedures, and • Restricting activities to duties that do not interfere with the attendant's primary responsibility to monitor and protect authorized entrants.
Assistance Tools	Standard – 29 CFR 1910.146 *Permit-required confined spaces.* Standard Appendix – 1910.146 Non-Mandatory Appendix F, *Rescue Team or Rescue Service Evaluation Criteria.* Interpretation Letter – May 9, 1994, Battalion Chief Chase Sargent, *Permit Required Confined Space Standard as it relates to rescue services.*

9.   29 CFR 1910.156 *Fire brigades*

When an employer establishes a fire brigade to respond to workplace fires, it must meet organizational, training, and personal protective equipment requirements. This section applies to fire brigades, industrial fire departments and private or contractual type fire departments. It does not apply to airport crash rescue or forest fire fighting operations.

Procedural, Program, and/or Equipment Requirements	Prepare and maintain a fire brigade written organizational statement. Document fire brigade member training information in the organizational statement. Ensure employees expected to fight fires are physically capable to perform assigned duties. Inspect and maintain fire fighting equipment annually. Inspect respirators and fire extinguishers monthly. Remove and replace damaged equipment. Supply protective clothing with components to protect the head, body, and extremities at no cost to the employee. Ensure fire brigade members are provided with and use compliant respirators.
Training Requirements	Provide training in the amount and frequency necessary to prepare members for their expected duties and any special hazards they may encounter. Ensure the quality of fire brigade training is equivalent to the training provided by the specified fire training schools referenced in the standard.
Assistance Tools	Standard – 29 CFR 1910.156 *Fire Brigades.* Supporting Statement for Paperwork Reduction Act 1995 Submissions – *Fire brigades (Organizational Statement).* Interpretation letter – February 22, 1991, Mr. Richard H. Timms, *Respirators for fire-fighters.*

Assistance Tools (Continued)	Interpretation Letter – April 26, 2002, Mr. Steve Boykin, *Training requirements for fire brigade members.*
	Interpretation Letter – June 20, 1997, Regional Administrators, *SCBA Cylinder Interchangeability.*
	National Fire Protection Agency (NFPA) Code – *Life Safety Code NFPA 101.*
	National Fire Protection Agency (NFPA) Code – *Standard on Comprehensive Occupational Medical Program for Fire Departments NFPA 1582.*

10. 29 CFR 1910.262 *Textiles*

This section applies to textile machinery, equipment, and other plant facility characteristics except processes used exclusively in synthetic fiber manufacturing.

Procedural, Program, and/or Equipment Requirements	Supply a copious and flowing supply of fresh, clean water wherever acids or caustics are used.
	When hazards are present or likely to be present, select and use PPE in accordance with 1910.132, 1910.133, and 1910.134.
Assistance Tools	Standard – 29 CFR 1910.262 *Textiles.*
	Standard – 29 CFR 1910.5(c) *Applicability of the Standards.*

11. 29 CFR 1910.266 *Logging operations*

Logging operations include felling and moving trees or logs from the stump to the delivery point. The risk of injury increases with dangerous environmental conditions and when worksites do not have immediate accessibility to health care facilities.

Procedural, Program, and/or Equipment Requirements	Provide sufficient and adequate first aid kits for worksites and transport vehicles. Provide sufficient kits based on the number of employees, anticipated hazards, and worksite isolation.
	Maintain contents of each first aid kit in a serviceable condition.
Training Requirements	Provide and keep current minimum first aid and CPR training for each supervisor and employee.

Assistance Tools	Standard – 29 CFR 1910.266 *Logging Operations.*
	Standard – 29 CFR 1910.266 Appendix A *First-Aid Kits (Mandatory).*
	Standard – 29 CFR 1910.5(c) *Applicability of the Standards.*
	OSHA Website Safety and Health Topics – *Logging.*
	E-Tools – *Logging eTool.*

12. 29 CFR 1910.268 *Telecommunications*

This section applies to all aspects of work performed at telecommunications centers and at telecommunications field installations. This includes outdoor and indoor locations.

Procedural, Program, and/or Equipment Requirements	Do not perform tree work during storm or emergency conditions. When an emergency condition develops due to tree operations, implement procedures to suspend work and notify the electric utility system operator/owner.
	If work includes entry into a manhole occupied jointly by telecommunication and electric utilities, or if there is a potential that a safety hazard exists, provide an employee who is immediately available to render first aid.
	Provide quick-drenching and/or eye-flushing facilities for battery handling areas. Provide first aid kits approved by a consulting physician, ensuring the kits are readily accessible, inspected monthly, and replenished as necessary.
Training Requirements	Provide employees with appropriate training on emergency situation procedures and first aid (including instruction in artificial respiration).
	Train employees working with storage batteries on emergency procedures for acid spills.
	Maintain proper training certifications for employment duration.
Assistance Tools	Standard – 29 CFR 1910.268 *Telecommunications.*

13. 29 CFR 1910.269 *Electric power generation, transmission and distribution*

This section covers the operation and maintenance of electric power generation, control, transformation, transmission, and distribution lines and equipment.

Procedural, Program, and/or Equipment Requirements	Ensure that an employee with training is immediately available outside an enclosed space with potential hazards and ready to give emergency assistance and first aid. If energized electric equipment is contained in a manhole where work is being performed, ensure that the attendant is also trained to provide CPR. Provide equipment to ensure the prompt and safe rescue of employees from enclosed spaces. Provide medical care and first aid as required in 29 CFR 1910.151(b) (**Note:** See Section I.A.3.). Place supplies in weatherproof containers if the supplies could be exposed to weather. Inspect and maintain first aid kits often enough, at least annually, to ensure replacement of needed or expired items. Provide water or showers for emergency use when chemically cleaning boilers and pressure vessels in power generating plants. Provide emergency repair kits near the shelter or enclosure for prompt repair of leaks in lines, equipment, or containers of chlorine systems.
Training Requirements	Train employees in emergency procedures applicable to their work, such as pole top and manhole rescue. Train sufficient employees in first aid and CPR, when working on or near exposed lines or equipment at 50 volts or more.
Assistance Tools	Standard – 29 CFR 1910.269 *Electric power generation, transmission, and distribution.* Interpretation letter – February 22, 1999, Richard S. Terrill, *CPR/first-aid training and working along provisions.* Interpretation letter – February 13, 1997, *Electric power generation, transmission, and distribution standard regarding pole-top rescue.*

14.   29 CFR 1910.272 *Grain handling facilities*

Grain handling facility regulations cover a wide range of grain handling operations and include emergency planning and training requirements. Some typical emergencies that may occur at these facilities include fires, explosions, and electrocutions.

Procedural, Program, and/or Equipment Requirements	Develop and implement an emergency action plan according to 29 CFR 1910.38 (**Note:** See Section I.B.1.). Provide two or more emergency escape routes from galleries or bin decks. Provide emergency escape route(s) for grain elevator tunnels. Provide a body harness and lifeline or boatswain's chair for entry into grain storage structures when the employee enters at or above the grain level. Ensure that a properly equipped observer maintains communication with an employee who enters a bin, silo, or tank. Provide rescue equipment designed for the storage structure.

Training Requirements	Train employees who serve as observers for entry into grain storage structures on rescue procedures, including notification for additional assistance.
	Explain the emergency action plan to contractors. Notify contractors of potential fire and explosion hazards related to their work and work area.
	Inform contractors performing work at the grain handling facility of known potential fire and explosion hazards related to the contractor's work and work area.
Assistance Tools	Standard – 29 CFR 1910.272 *Grain handling facilities.*
	Standard – 29 CFR 1910.272 Appendix A *Grain handling facilities.*
	OSHA Safety and Health Topics – *Grain Handling.*
	NIOSH ALERT – July 1986, DHHS (NIOSH) Publication No. 86-118, *Preventing Fatalities Due to Fires and Explosions in Oxygen-Limiting Silos.*
	National Agriculture Safety Database – Dawna L. Cyr and Steven B. Johnson, Ph.D. University of Maine *Grain Storage Safety.*

15. 29 CFR 1910 Subpart T *Diving Operations*
(*29 CFR 1910.104 Scope and application,*
1910.410 Qualifications of dive team,
1910.420 Safe practice manual,
1910.421 Pre-dive procedures, and
1910.422 Procedures during dive)

These standards cover diving and related support operations conducted in connection with all types of work and employments, including general industry, construction, ship repairing, shipbuilding, shipbreaking, and longshoring. They include requirements for a safe practices manual, including emergency procedures. These standards also require the posting of emergency information, the availability of first aid kit(s), emergency communication equipment, and employee CPR and emergency training.

Procedural, Program, and/or Equipment Requirements	Develop and maintain a safe practices manual that includes emergency procedures for fire, equipment failure, adverse environmental conditions, and medical illness and injury for each diving mode. Make the manual available at the dive location to each dive team member.
	Ensure that the planning of a diving operation includes an assessment of emergency procedures.
	Prior to each diving operation, ensure that a list of telephone or call numbers for the following is kept at the dive location:
	• An operational decompression chamber (if not at the dive location),
	• Accessible hospitals,
	• Available physicians,
	• Available means of transportation, and
	• The nearest U.S. Coast Guard Rescue Coordination Center.

Procedural, Program, and/or Equipment Requirements (Continued)	Provide at the dive location a first aid kit appropriate for the diving operation and approved by a physician. When used in a decompression chamber or bell, ensure the first aid kit is suitable for use under hyperbaric conditions.
	Provide an American Red Cross standard first aid handbook or equivalent, and a bag-type manual resuscitator with transparent mask and tubing at the dive location.
	Provide an operational, two-way communication system at the dive location for obtaining emergency assistance.
Training Requirements	Ensure that dive team members have experience and/or provide training in diving operations and emergency procedures.
	Ensure that all dive team members are trained in CPR and first aid (American Red Cross standard course or equivalent).
Assistance Tools	Standard – 29 CFR 1910.401 *Scope and application.*
	Standard – 29 CFR 1910.410 *Qualifications of dive team.*
	Standard – 29 CFR 1910.420 *Safe practice manual.*
	Standard – 29 CFR 1910.421 *Pre-dive procedures.*
	Standard – 29 CFR 1910.422 *Procedures during dive.*
	Directive – STD 01-17-001 – 29 CFR 1910.401-1910.441, Subpart T, - Commercial Diving Operations.
	OSHA Website Safety and Health Topics – *Commercial Diving.*

16. **29 CFR 1910.1003** *13 Carcinogens (4-Nitrobiphenyl, etc.);*
1910.1004 alpha-Naphthylamine,
1910.1006 Methyl chloromethyl ether,
1910.1007 3,3'-Dichlorobenzidine (and its salts),
1910.1008 bis-Chloromethyl ether,
1910.1009 beta-Naphthylamine,
1910.1010 Benzidine,
1910.1011 4-Aminodiphenyl,
1910.1012 Ethyleneimine,
1910.1013 beta-Propiolactone,
1910.1014 2-Acetylaminofluorene,
1910.1015 4-Dimethylaminoazobenzene, and/or
1910.1016 N-Nitrosodimethylamine

This standard covers any area in which the 13 carcinogens identified in the standard are manufactured, processed, repackaged, released, handled, or stored. The standard requires that an employer establish a regulated area where any of the 13 carcinogens are being handled and includes requirements addressing emergency releases in these areas. An emergency means an unforeseen circumstance or set of circumstances resulting in a carcinogen release that may result in employee exposure to or contact with the material.

Procedural, Program, and/or Equipment Requirements	Post appropriate signs at regulated area entrances and exits.
	Prescribe and post specific emergency procedures.
	Provide emergency showers and eyewash fountains near, within sight of, and on the same level where a direct exposure to Ethyleneimine or beta-Propiolactone would be most likely as a result of equipment failure or improper work practice.
	Evacuate areas where an emergency release has occurred. Correct the hazardous conditions and decontaminate the area before restarting normal operations.
	Ensure that employee(s) who were exposed shower as soon as possible.
	Provide special medical surveillance by a physician within 24 hours for employees located in an area where an emergency release has occurred.
	Report all releases that may expose employees to the OSHA Area Director within 24 hours. File a written report to the nearest OSHA Area Director within 15 calendar days.
Training Requirements	Before an employee is authorized to enter a regulated area provide, and review at least annually, training on the purpose and his or her role in emergency procedures, how to recognize situations that may result in a carcinogen release, and specific first aid care.
	Familiarize and rehearse with employees the specific emergency procedures that are prescribed and posted.
	Ensure that employees who must wear respiratory protection, including those who do not evacuate but stay to handle emergencies, receive training consistent with 29 CFR 1910.134.
Assistance Tools	Standard – 29 CFR 1910.1003 *13 Carcinogens (1910.1004-1016)*.
	National Institute for Occupational Safety and Health (NIOSH) – *Pocket Guide to Hazardous Chemicals*.
	OSHA Website Safety and Health Topics – *Carcinogens*.

17. 29 CFR 1910.1017 *Vinyl chloride*

This section applies to a variety of vinyl chloride or polyvinyl chloride operations and uses but does not apply to the handling or use of fabricated products made of polyvinyl chloride. Emergencies involving vinyl chloride occur when operations are likely to or actually result in a massive vinyl chloride release.

Procedural, Program, and/or Equipment Requirements	Post appropriate signs at entrances to regulated areas, areas containing hazardous operations, or where an emergency exists.
	For each facility using vinyl chloride as a liquid or compressed gas, develop a written operational plan for emergencies. Ensure that the plan addresses hazardous operations, hazardous release correction, and evacuation of the release area.
	Provide protective equipment for those working in hazardous areas and hazardous release areas.
	Provide appropriate medical surveillance to an employee exposed to an emergency.
	Report all emergencies to the OSHA Area Director within 24 hours.
Training Requirements	Include emergency procedures, how to recognize conditions that may result in a vinyl chloride release, and fire hazards and prevention in the employee training program.
	Ensure that employees who must wear respiratory protection, including those who do not evacuate but stay to handle emergencies, receive training consistent with 29 CFR 1910.134.
Assistance Tools	Standard – 29 CFR 1910.1017 *Vinyl chloride*.
	Interpretation letter – March 10, 1986, Mr. Donald G. Mader, *Definitions of "massive release", "equipment failure", and "emergency" under the vinyl chloride standard.*

18.   29 CFR 1910.1027 *Cadmium*

This standard applies to all occupational exposures to cadmium and cadmium compounds, in all forms. The standard requires the development of a written plan for emergencies involving substantial releases of airborne cadmium and includes requirements for employee training on emergencies and medical examinations.

Procedural, Program, and/or Equipment Requirements	Develop and implement a written plan for dealing with emergency situations involving substantial releases of airborne cadmium. At a minimum, the plan must include
	• Provisions for the use of appropriate respirators and PPE, and
	• Restrictions for employees not essential to correcting the emergency situation from the area and normal operations halted in that area until the emergency is abated.
	Select and provide appropriate respirators for emergencies.
	Provide required medical examinations as soon as possible to any employee who may have been acutely exposed to cadmium because of an emergency.

Training Requirements	Provide training, including training on emergency procedures, prior to or at the time of initial assignment to a job involving potential exposure to cadmium and at least annually thereafter.
	Ensure employees who must wear respiratory protection, including those who do not evacuate but stay to handle emergencies, receive training consistent with 29 CFR 1910.134.
Assistance Tools	Standard – 29 CFR 1910.1027 *Cadmium*.
	Standard Appendix – 1910.1027 Appendix A, *Substance safety data sheet – Cadmium*.

19. 29 CFR 1910.1028 *Benzene*

This standard covers benzene, in various forms, with exception to some fuels, certain storage facilities, materials with extremely small concentrations, and specific operations using benzene. Situations that are considered emergencies involving benzene include, but are not limited to, equipment failure, rupture of containers, or failure of control equipment, which may or does result in an unexpected significant benzene release.

Procedural, Program, and/or Equipment Requirements	Post signs at entrances to regulated areas.
	Select and provide appropriate respirators for emergencies.
	Whenever spills, leaks, ruptures, or other breakdowns occur that may lead to employee exposure, monitor (using area or personal sampling) after the cleanup of the spill or repair of the leak, rupture, or other breakdown to ensure that exposures have returned to the level that existed prior to the incident.
	Provide medical surveillance, required urine and blood analysis, and follow-up testing and consultation, as designated.
Training Requirements	Train employees on the applicable requirements in 29 CFR 1910.1200 (Hazard communication standard), the procedural and equipment requirements in 1910.1028, and respiratory protection.
Assistance Tools	Standard – 29 CFR 1910.1028 *Benzene*.
	Standard Appendix – 1910.1028 Appendix A, *Substance safety data sheet, Benzene*.

20. 29 CFR 1910.1029 *Coke oven emissions*

Coke oven emissions are produced by the destructive distillation or carbonization of coal. Exceptions to applying this standard may occur when other Federal agencies exercise statutory authority that affects occupational safety and health. An emergency includes, but is not limited to, equipment failure that is likely to, or does, result in any massive coke oven emission release.

Procedural, Program, and/or Equipment Requirements	Post applicable signs in regulated areas. Select and provide appropriate respirators for emergencies. Do not begin the next coking cycle following an emergency until the cause of the emergency is determined and corrected, unless the cycle is necessary to determine the cause of the emergency.
Training Requirements	Include a review of emergency procedures and respirator use in the training program.
Assistance Tools	Standard – 29 CFR 1910.1029 *Coke oven emissions*.

21. 29 CFR 1910.1044 *1,2-dibromo-3-chloropropane*

This section applies to occupational exposure to 1,2-dibromo-3-chloropropane (DBCP) except when used as a fertilizer or when sealed appropriately in a container. An emergency includes, but is not limited to, equipment failure, rupture of containers, or failure of control equipment which may, or does, result in an unexpected release of DBCP.

Procedural, Program, and/or Equipment Requirements	Post applicable signs that indicate all regulated areas. Develop, and implement as necessary, a written plan for emergencies for each workplace containing DBCP. Select and provide appropriate respirators, protective clothing and equipment for emergencies. Evacuate employees not engaged in responding to the emergency and do not resume normal operations until the emergency is abated. Install and maintain an alarm for alerting employees in case of a DBCP emergency. Provide medical surveillance and exposure monitoring when employees are exposed during a DBCP emergency.

Training Requirements	Inform employees about the emergency and first aid procedures in Appendix A.
	Ensure that employee training covers a review of 29 CFR 1910.1044, including emergency requirements.
	Ensure that employees who must wear respiratory protection, including those who do not evacuate but stay to handle emergencies, receive training consistent with 29 CFR 1910.134.
Assistance Tools	Standard – 29 CFR 1910.1044 *1,2-dibromo-3-chloropropane.*
	Standard Appendix – 1910.1044 Appendix A, *Substance safety data sheet for DBCP.*
	Standard Appendix – 1910.1044 Appendix B, *Substance technical guidelines for DBCP.*

22.   29 CFR 1910.1045 *Acrylonitrile*

This section applies to occupational exposures to acrylonitrile (AN). Exceptions apply to some uses, handling, emissions, and temperatures. Any unexpected massive AN release is considered an emergency.

Procedural, Program, and/or Equipment Requirements	Identify the rooms in the workplace that contain AN by posting appropriate signs.
	Select and provide appropriate respirators for emergencies.
	Develop, and implement as necessary, a written plan for emergencies involving AN.
	Install and maintain an alarm for alerting employees in case of an AN emergency.
	Evacuate employees not engaged in correcting the emergency and do not allow their return until the emergency is abated.
	Report all AN emergencies to the OSHA Area Office within 72 hours.
Training Requirements	Include information about the emergency and first aid procedures in Appendix A.
	Provide emergency procedure training upon initial assignment and at least annually thereafter.
	Ensure that employees who must wear respiratory protection, including those who do not evacuate but stay to handle emergencies, receive training consistent with 29 CFR 1910.134.
Assistance Tools	Standard – 29 CFR 1910.1045 *Acrylonitrile.*
	Standard Appendix – 1910.1045 Appendix A, *Substance safety data sheet for acrylonitrile.*

23.   29 CFR 1910.1047 *Ethylene oxide*

Ethylene oxide (EtO) possesses several physical and health hazards that merit special attention. This section applies to all occupational exposures to ethylene oxide (EtO) except some processes, uses, or handling of products containing EtO. A situation is an emergency when an unexpected significant release of EtO is likely to or does occur. This standard also applies to EtO used in emergency response efforts to clean up anthrax contaminated sites.

Procedural, Program, and/or Equipment Requirements	Post applicable signs that identify the rooms where EtO is used. Select and provide appropriate respirators for emergencies. Develop, and implement as necessary, a written plan for emergencies involving EtO. Include the elements required by 29 CFR 1910.38 and 1910.39. Install and maintain a general alarm to promptly alert employees of an EtO emergency and evacuate all employees from the area in an emergency situation. Provide medical exams and consultations to employees exposed during an EtO emergency.
Training Requirements	Initially, and at least annually, train employees in emergency EtO procedures. Inform applicable employees about the emergency and first aid procedures in Appendix A. Train employees on how to detect workplace EtO releases. Ensure that employees who must wear respiratory protection, including those who do not evacuate but stay to handle emergencies, receive training consistent with 29 CFR 1910.134.
Assistance Tools	Standard – 29 CFR 1910.1047 *Ethylene oxide.* Standard Appendix – 29 CFR 1910.1047 Appendix A, *Substance safety data sheet for ethylene oxide (non-mandatory).* Interpretation Letter – December 11, 1998, Mr. Darrel Giraud, *Use of ethylene oxide alarm systems with sensors.*

24.   29 CFR 1910.1048 *Formaldehyde*

This standard applies to all occupational exposures to formaldehyde. An emergency includes, but is not limited to, equipment failure, rupture of containers, or failure of control equipment that results in an uncontrolled release of formaldehyde in a significant amount.

Procedural, Program, and/or Equipment Requirements	Ensure that procedures are adopted and implemented to minimize injury and loss of life for each workplace, where an emergency involving formaldehyde is a possibility. Select and provide appropriate respirators for emergencies. Provide full body protection protective clothing for emergency reentry into areas of unknown concentration. Provide eyewash facilities in areas based on exposure probability. For all employees exposed to formaldehyde during an emergency, make medical examinations and surveillance available, and provide details about the exposure to the physician as soon as possible.
Training Requirements	Train employees in emergency procedures, including the specific duties for each employee during an emergency. Provide instruction for handling spills and cleanup procedures. Ensure that employees who must wear respiratory protection, including those who do not evacuate but stay to handle emergencies, receive training consistent with 29 CFR 1910.134.
Assistance Tools	Standard – 29 CFR 1910.1048 *Formaldehyde*. Standard Appendix – 29 CFR 1910.1048 Appendix C, *Medical surveillance – Formaldehyde*. Interpretation Letter – December 12, 1989, Mr. Thomas J. Dufficy, *Requirements under the formaldehyde standard for quick drench showers, eye wash facilities, emergency plans and sampling*.

25.   29 CFR 1910.1050 *Methylenedianiline*

This section covers general industry occupational exposures to Methylenedianiline (MDA), except as provided by the standard. The standard requires a written plan for emergencies and addresses emergency alerting means, protective equipment, and medical surveillance. "Emergency" means any occurrence such as, but not limited to, equipment failure, rupture of containers, or failure of control equipment that results in an unexpected and potentially hazardous release of MDA.

Procedural, Program, and/or Equipment Requirements	Develop and implement a written plan for emergency situations where there is a possibility of an emergency. At a minimum, the plan must • Specifically provide that employees engaged in correcting emergency conditions shall be equipped with the appropriate PPE and clothing until the emergency is abated. • Specifically include provisions for alerting and evacuating affected employees. • Include elements prescribed in Emergency action plans (29 CFR 1910.38) and Fire prevention plans (29 CFR 1910.39).

Procedural, Program, and/or Equipment Requirements (Continued)	Where there is the possibility of employee exposure to MDA due to an emergency, provide means to promptly alert employees who have the potential to be directly exposed.
	Ensure that employees not engaged in correcting emergency conditions are immediately evacuated in the event of an emergency.
	Select and provide appropriate respirators for use during emergencies.
	Make available a medical surveillance program, as provided by the standard, for employees exposed to MDA during an emergency situation.
Training Requirements	Provide employees with information and training on MDA, in accordance with 29 CFR 1910.1200(h), at the time of initial assignment and at least annually thereafter.
	Ensure employees who must wear respiratory protection, including those who do not evacuate but stay to handle emergencies, receive training consistent with 29 CFR 1910.134.
Assistance Tools	Standard – 29 CFR 1910.1050 *Methylenedianiline*.
	Standard Appendix – 1910.1050 Appendix A, *Substance data sheet, for 4,4'-Methylenedianiline*.

26. 29 CFR 1910.1051 *1,3-Butadiene*

This section applies to all occupational exposures to 1,3-Butadiene (BD), except as provided by the standard. The standard requires a written plan for emergencies and addresses protective equipment and medical surveillance. "Emergency situation" means any occurrence such as, but not limited to, equipment failure, rupture of containers, or failure of control equipment that may or does result in an uncontrolled significant release of BD.

Procedural, Program, and/or Equipment Requirements	Develop and implement a written plan for emergency situations where there is a possibility of an emergency. At a minimum, the plan must include applicable elements prescribed in
	• Emergency action plans (29 CFR 1910.38),
	• Fire prevention plans (29 CFR 1910.39), and
	• Hazardous waste operations and emergency response (29 CFR 1910.120).
	Make available a medical screening and surveillance program, as provided by the standard, for employees exposed to BD during an emergency situation. Ensure that medical screening is conducted following an emergency situation as quickly as possible, but not later than 48 hours after exposure.
	Select and provide appropriate respirators for use during emergencies.

Training Requirements	Provide training, including training on emergency procedures, prior to or at the time of initial assignment to a job potentially involving exposure to BD at or above the action level or short-term exposure limit and at least annually thereafter.
	Ensure that employees who must wear respiratory protection, including those who do not evacuate but stay to handle emergencies, receive training consistent with 29 CFR 1910.134.
Assistance Tools	Standard – 29 CFR 1910.1051 *1,3 Butadiene*.
	Standard Appendix – 1910.1051 Appendix A – *Substance safety data sheet for 1,3-Butadiene*.
	Directive – CPL 02-02-066 – *1,3-Butadiene*.

27.   29 CFR 1910.1052 *Methylene Chloride*

This standard applies to all occupational exposures to methylene chloride (MC). It establishes requirements for employers to control occupational exposure to MC and addresses protective equipment, eyewash facilities, and medical surveillance for emergencies. "Emergency" means any occurrence, such as, but not limited to, equipment failure, rupture of containers, or failure of control equipment, which results, or is likely to result in an uncontrolled release of MC.

Procedural, Program, and/or Equipment Requirements	Ensure that incidental leaks are repaired and that incidental spills are promptly cleaned up by employees who use the appropriate personal protective equipment and are trained in proper methods of cleanup. If employees respond to cleanup an emergency release of MC, implement an emergency response as described in 29 CFR 1910.120(q).
	Select and provide appropriate respirators for use during emergencies.
	Provide within the immediate work area and ensure that affected employees use appropriate emergency eyewash facilities if it is reasonably foreseeable that an employee's eyes may contact solutions containing 0.1 percent or greater MC (for example through splashes, spills, or improper work practices).
	Provide emergency medical surveillance, treatment, and decontamination, as provided by the standard, for employees exposed to MC during an emergency.
Training Requirements	Provide training and information for each affected employee prior to or at the time of initial assignment to a job involving potential exposure to MC.
	Ensure that employees who must wear respiratory protection, including those who do not evacuate but stay to handle emergencies, receive training consistent with 29 CFR 1910.134.

Assistance Tools	Standard – 29 CFR 1910.1052 *Methylene Chloride.*
	Standard Appendix – 1910.1052 Appendix A, *Substance Safety Data Sheet and Technical Guidelines for Methylene Chloride.*
	Directive – CPL 02-02-070 – *Inspection Procedures for Occupational Exposure to Methylene Chloride Final Rule 29 CFR Part 1910.1052, 29 CFR Part 1915.1052 and 29 CFR 1926.1152.*

28. 29 CFR 1910.1450 *Occupational exposure to hazardous chemicals in laboratories*

This standard covers the laboratory use of hazardous chemicals and supercedes the health standards of 29 CFR 1910 Subpart Z, with a few exceptions for employee exposure limits, eye and skin contact, and action levels as it relates to medical surveillance. Emergencies in labs include occurrences that result in an uncontrolled release of a hazardous chemical into the workplace.

Procedural, Program, and/or Equipment Requirements	Include hazard determination and controls in the chemical hygiene plan.
	When a spill, leak, explosion, or other event occurs, determine the need for a medical examination by providing affected employees the opportunity for medical consultation.
Training Requirements	Provide training on how to detect the presence or release of a hazardous chemical.
	Train employees in specific emergency procedures.
	Ensure that employees who must wear respiratory protection, including those who do not evacuate but stay to handle emergencies, receive training consistent with 29 CFR 1910.134.
Assistance Tools	Standard – 29 CFR 1910.1450 *Occupational exposure to hazardous chemicals in laboratories.*
	Standard Appendix – 29 CFR 1910.1450 Appendix A, *National Research Council Recommendations Concerning Chemical Hygiene in Laboratories (Non-Mandatory).*

D. Requirements that Support Emergency Response and Preparedness

1. 29 CFR 1910.132 *General requirements (Personal Protective Equipment)*

This standard applies to PPE for eyes, face, head, and extremities, protective clothing; respiratory devices, and protective shields and barriers. Emergency situations often require PPE and must meet these general requirements when not addressed in a hazard- or industry-specific standard.

Procedural, Program, and/or Equipment Requirements	Assess the workplace for hazards that are present or likely to be present. Select and ensure the use of PPE based on the workplace assessment.
Training Requirements	Provide PPE training to all employees required to use PPE. Retrain employees when it is believed the employee does not have the understanding or skill to properly use the PPE. Verify that each affected employee has received and understood the required training through a written certification.
Assistance Tools	Standard – 29 CFR 1910.132 *General requirements (Personal Protective Equipment)*. Standard Appendix – 29 CFR 1910 Subpart I Appendix B, *Non-mandatory Compliance Guidelines for Hazard Assessment and Personal Protective Equipment Selection*. Fact Sheet – OSHA Fact Sheet, *Personal Protective Equipment*. Other Agency Guidance – Center for Disease Control, *Personal Protective Equipment Program*. Other Agency Guidance – NIOSH, *Recommendations for Chemical Protective Clothing*.

2.   29 CFR 1910.134 *Respiratory protection*

The standard covers respirator use when atmospheric contamination cannot be reduced through effective engineering controls. An emergency situation means any occurrence such as, but not limited to, equipment failure, rupture of containers, or failure of control equipment that may or does result in an uncontrolled significant release of an airborne contaminant.

Procedural, Program, and/or Equipment Requirements	Select and provide respirators suitable for the intended purpose. When respirators are required, establish and implement a written respiratory protection program that includes procedures for proper respirator use in emergency situations. Update the program when changes in workplace conditions affect respirator use. Clean and disinfect emergency respirators after each use. Ensure that emergency respirators are properly stored and inspected. Certify emergency-only respirators by a certification tag or other proper documentation method. For entry into Immediately Dangerous to Life and Health (IDLH) environments, provide retrieval equipment or equivalent means for rescue of employees. Maintain required personnel and communications for emergency rescue. For interior structural firefighting, ensure that at least two employees who remain in contact with one another enter the structure.

Procedural, Program, and/or Equipment Requirements (Continued)	Provide sufficient standby personnel when employees enter IDLH environments. During interior structural firefighting, provide at least two standby personnel. Provide and ensure the use of self-contained breathing apparatuses during interior structural firefighting.
Training Requirements	Train, at least annually, all employees required to use a respirator on how to use the respirator effectively in emergency situations, including situations in which the respirator malfunctions. Provide training on the respiratory hazards employees may potentially be exposed to in emergency situations. Train and equip employees who provide emergency rescue in IDLH atmospheres.
Assistance Tools	Standard – 29 CFR 1910.134 *Respiratory protection.* Standard Appendix – 29 CFR 1910.134 Appendix B, *Respirator Cleaning Procedures (Mandatory).* Publication – *Questions and Answers on the Respiratory Protection Standard.* Publication – *Small Entity Compliance Guide for the Revised Respiratory Protection Standard.* E-Tools – *Respiratory Protection.* Interpretation Letter – April 29, 1998, J. Curtis Varone, Esq., *Two-in/two-out procedure in firefighting/IDLH environments.*

3.   29 CFR 1910.1000 *Air contaminants*

This standard establishes exposure limits for air contaminants. The standard includes ceiling concentrations and 8-hour time-weighted average limits for contaminants. It also provides a designation when exposure to the skin is a significant route of exposure. *Note:* The standard also includes limits for "Acceptable maximum peak above the acceptable ceiling concentration for an 8-hour shift" for some contaminants (Table Z-2). In addition, other OSHA standards include short-term exposure limits for some contaminants.

Procedural, Program, and/or Equipment Requirements	Ensure that employee exposures do not exceed the limits provided by the standard. Exposures must be limited through engineering controls, administrative controls, and, as a last resort, PPE.

Assistance Tools	Standard – 29 CFR 1910.1000 *Air contaminants*.
	Standard Appendix – 29 CFR 1910.1000 TABLE Z-1, *Limits for Air Contaminants*.
	Standard Appendix – 29 CFR 1910.1000 TABLE Z-2.
	Standard Appendix – 29 CFR 1910.1000 TABLE Z-3, *Mineral Dusts*.

4. 29 CFR 1910.1030 *Bloodborne pathogens*

This section applies to all occupational exposure to blood or other potentially infectious materials. Occupational exposure means reasonably anticipated contact with blood or other potentially infectious materials that may result from the performance of an employee's duties. Employees who are responsible for rendering first aid or medical assistance as part of their job duties are covered by the protections of the standard.

Procedural, Program, and/or Equipment Requirements	Establish and maintain a written Exposure Control Plan when there is occupational exposure to blood or other potentially infectious materials. This plan must be designed to eliminate or minimize employee exposure to bloodborne pathogens.
	Prepare an exposure determination for job classifications having occupational exposure.
	Provide appropriate PPE when employee exposure remains after the institution of engineering and work practice controls.
	Provide hepatitis B vaccine and vaccination series to all employees who have occupational exposure. Provide post-exposure evaluation and follow-up to all employees who have had an exposure incident in accordance with the Centers for Disease Control guidelines current at the time of the evaluation or procedure.
Training Requirements	Provide initial and annual bloodborne pathogens training to employees with occupational exposure.
	Provide information on the appropriate actions to take and persons to contact in the event of an emergency involving contact with blood or other potentially infectious materials.
Assistance Tools	Standard – 29 CFR 1910.1030 *Bloodborne Pathogens*.
	Directive – CPL 02-02-069 – *Enforcement Procedures for the Occupational Exposure to Bloodborne Pathogens*.
	Interpretation – February 1, 1993, *Most frequently asked questions concerning the bloodborne pathogens standard*.

5. 29 CFR 1910.1200 *Hazard communication*

The hazard communication standard is intended to ensure that the hazards of all chemicals produced or imported are evaluated and that information concerning these hazards is transmitted to employers and employees. This standard includes hazardous chemicals that employees may be exposed to in a foreseeable emergency.

Procedural, Program, and/or Equipment Requirements	Chemical manufacturers and importers must obtain or develop a material safety data sheet that includes emergency and first aid procedures for each hazardous chemical they produce or import.
	Develop and implement a hazard communication program. Ensure that material safety data sheets for each hazardous chemical used and the hazard communication program are available to workers in the workplace.
	For employees that travel between workplaces during a workshift, ensure that employees can immediately obtain the required information in an emergency.
Training Requirements	Provide training and information to employees on how to identify the release of hazardous chemicals in the work area, protect themselves from exposure, and implement emergency procedures.
Assistance Tools	Standard – 29 CFR 1910.1200 *Hazard communication.*
	Directive – CPL 02-02-038 – *Inspection Procedures for the Hazard Communication Standard.*
	Frequently Asked Questions – *Hazard Communication (HAZCOM).*

NOTE: In addition to the General Industry standards highlighted in this publication, the following standards also contain limited emergency-related requirements: 29 CFR 1910.68 Manlifts; 1910.1001 Asbestos; 1910.1018 Arsenic; and 1910.1096 Ionizing radiation.

II. Shipyard Employment (29 CFR 1915) Requirements for Emergency Response and Preparedness

A. General Requirements for Workplaces

1. 29 CFR 1915.52 *Fire prevention*

This standard covers fire prevention during welding, cutting, and heating operations for shipyard employment. It contains requirements to reduce fire potential, provide fire extinguishing equipment, and ensure that sufficient people are informed and available to assist in identifying and controlling fire hazards.

Procedural, Program, and/or Equipment Requirements	For ship building and repairing, provide sufficient additional personnel (fire watch personnel) for welding, cutting, and heating operations when necessary to guard against fire during and after those operations.
	Provide fire extinguishing equipment in ship breaking work areas that is suitable for the fire hazards and ready for use.
Training Requirements	Instruct fire watch personnel of potential fire hazards and on the use of fire fighting equipment.
	Instruct all ship breaking personnel expected to contain fires as to the fire hazards and the use of fire fighting equipment.
Assistance Tools	Standard – 29 CFR 1915.52 *Fire Prevention*.
	E-Tools – *Shipyard Employment – Ship Repair*.

2. 29 CFR 1915.98 *First aid*

This standard covers first aid requirements for shipyard employment. It contains requirements to ensure the availability of first aid equipment and employee(s) qualified to provide first aid.

Procedural, Program, and/or Equipment Requirements	Unless a first aid room or qualified attendant is close at hand to render care, provide an adequate first aid kit where work is being performed. Kits must be checked at least weekly to ensure they are sufficiently stocked.
	When 10 or more employees are working at a location, ensure a stretcher(s) is available and kept close to the vessels. This is not a requirement if available ambulance services are known to carry such stretchers.
Training Requirements	Ensure that at least one employee, close at hand, is qualified to render first aid.
Assistance Tools	Standard – 29 CFR 1915.98 *First aid*.
	E-Tools – *Shipyard Employment – Ship Repair*.

B. Additional Requirements for Workplaces Referenced in Other Requirements

There are no additional requirements for workplaces referenced in other requirements.

C. Additional Requirements for Specific Workplaces/Operations

1.   29 CFR 1915.12 *Diving Operations*

See Section I.C.15. (29 CFR 1910 Subpart T).

2.   29 CFR 1915.1003 *13 Carcinogens (4-Nitrobiphenyl, etc.);*
1915.1004 alpha-Naphthylamine,
1915.1006 Methyl chloromethyl ether,
1915.1007 3,3'-Dichlorobenzidine (and its salts),
1915.1008 bis-Chloromethyl ether,
1915.1009 beta-Naphthylamine,
19100.1010 Benzidine,
1910.1011 4-Aminodiphenyl,
1915.1012 Ethyleneimine,
1910.1013 beta-Propiolactone,
1910.1014 2-Acetylaminofluorene,
1915.1015 4-Dimethylaminoazobenzene, and/or
1915.1016 N-Nitrosodimethylamine.

See Section I.C.16. (29 CFR 1910.1003).

3.   29 CFR 1915.1017 *Vinyl chloride*

See Section I.C.17. (29 CFR 1910.1017).

4.   29 CFR 1915.1027 *Cadmium*

See Section I.C.18. (29 CFR 1910.1027).

5.   29 CFR 1915.1028 *Benzene*

See Section I.C.19. (29 CFR 1910.1028).

6.   29 CFR 1915.1044 *1,2-dibromo-3-chloropropane*

See Section I.C.21. (29 CFR 1910.1044).

7.   29 CFR 1915.1045 *Acrylonitrile*

See Section I.C.22. (29 CFR 1910.1045).

8.   29 CFR 1915.1047 *Ethylene oxide*

See Section I.C.23. (29 CFR 1910.1047).

9.   29 CFR 1915.1048 *Formaldehyde*

See Section I.C.24. (29 CFR 1910.1048).

10.   29 CFR 1915.1050 *Methylenedianiline*

See Section I.C.25. (29 CFR 1910.1050).

11.   29 CFR 1915.1052 *Methylene Chloride*

See Section I.C.27. (29 CFR 1910.1052).

12.   29 CFR 1915.1450 *Occupational exposure to hazardous chemicals in laboratories*

See Section I.C.28. (29 CFR 1910.1450).

D. Requirements that Support Emergency Response and Preparedness

1.   29 CFR 1915.152 *General requirements (Personal Protective Equipment)*

This standard covers the general requirements for evaluating the need for PPE, selecting the proper equipment, training employees on proper use, and ensuring that PPE is used by employees.

Procedural, Program, and/or Equipment Requirements	Assess work activities to determine if any hazards require the use of PPE, and document that hazard assessment.
	Select, provide, and ensure the use of appropriate PPE for each employee who is exposed to work hazards requiring PPE.
Training Requirements	Inform affected employees of the PPE selected based on the hazard assessment.
	Train each employee required to use PPE to understand when and what PPE is necessary; how to put on and remove PPE; how to wear and adjust PPE; the limitations and useful life of equipment; and the care, maintenance, and disposal of PPE.
	Employees must demonstrate the ability to use PPE prior to performing work requiring its use.
	Retrain employees who don't understand or display the skills necessary to properly use PPE. Changes in an employee's work task or duties, changes in the types of PPE used, and indications that an employee has not retained the knowledge to properly use PPE require retraining.
	Document all employee training with the date, employee's name, and type of training.
Assistance Tools	Standard – 29 CFR 1915.152 *General requirements (Personal Protective Equipment)*.
	E-Tools – *Shipyard Employment – Ship Repair*.

2.   29 CFR 1915.154 *Respiratory protection*

See Section I.D.2. (29 CFR 1910.134).

3.   29 CFR 1915.1000 *Air contaminants*

This standard establishes employee exposure limits for air contaminants. The standard includes ceiling limits and 8-hour time-weighted average limits for contaminants.

Procedural, Program, and/or Equipment Requirements	Ensure that employee exposures do not exceed the limits provided by the standard. Exposures should be limited through engineering controls, administrative controls, and, as a last resort, PPE.
Assistance Tools	Standard – 29 CFR 1915.1000 *Air contaminants*.

4.   29 CFR 1915.1030 *Bloodborne pathogens*

See Section I.D.4. (29 CFR 1910.1030).

5.   29 CFR 1915.1200 *Hazard communication*

See Section I.D.5. (29 CFR 1910.1200).

NOTE: In addition to the shipyard employment standards highlighted in this publication, the following standards also contain limited emergency-related requirements: 29 CFR 1915.12 Precautions and the order of testing before entering confined and enclosed spaces and other dangerous atmospheres; and 1915.92 Illumination.

III. Marine Terminals (29 CFR 1917) Requirements for Emergency Response and Preparedness

A. General Requirements for Workplaces

1. 29 CFR 1917.22 *Hazardous cargo*

This standard covers hazardous cargo in cargo handling operations. It addresses hazard identification and awareness, leak and spill procedures, and employee protection.

Procedural, Program, and/or Equipment Requirements	Prior to cargo handling, determine if hazardous cargo will be handled and the nature of the hazards.
	Remove employees from areas of a hazardous cargo spill or leak until the specific hazards have been identified.
	Once the hazards of spilled hazardous cargo have been identified, provide any equipment, clothing, and ventilation and fire protection equipment necessary to eliminate or protect against the hazard. Actual cleanup or disposal work shall be conducted under the supervision of a designated person.
Training Requirements	Inform employees of potential cargo hazards and precautions to protect themselves.
	Instruct employees to give notification in the case of spills or leaks and ensure that employees are informed of safe spill cleanup and container disposal methods.
Assistance Tools	Standard – 29 CFR 1917.22 *Hazardous cargo*.

2. 29 CFR 1917.23 *Hazardous atmospheres and substances*

This standard covers areas where the employer knows, or has reason to believe, that a hazardous atmosphere or substance may exist. Requirements cover hazard determination, testing during ventilation, and entry into areas containing hazardous atmospheres.

Procedural, Program, and/or Equipment Requirements	Protect persons entering a space containing a hazardous atmosphere by testing the atmosphere and providing appropriate respiratory and emergency protective equipment.
	Except for emergency or rescue operations, do not permit employees to enter into any atmosphere which has been identified as flammable or oxygen deficient (less than 19.5 percent oxygen).
	Standby observers must continuously monitor the activities of employees who enter an area containing a hazardous atmosphere.
	Post signs at entry to spaces with hazardous, flammable, or oxygen-deficient atmospheres to prevent inadvertent entry.
Training Requirements	Provide instruction to persons entering a space containing a hazardous atmosphere regarding the hazards, precautions to be taken, and the use of protective and emergency equipment. Standby observers must also be instructed similarly.

Training Requirements (Continued)	In emergency or rescue operations where entry into flammable or oxygen-deficient atmospheres is necessary, train employees as to the hazards and the use of self-contained breathing apparatus (SCBAs).
Assistance Tools	Standard – 29 CFR 1917.23 *Hazardous atmospheres and substances.* Standard – 29 CFR 1917.152 *Welding, cutting and heating (hot work).*

3.   29 CFR 1917.26 *First aid and lifesaving facilities*

This standard includes the requirements for first aid, stretchers, life rings, and communication for marine terminals.

Procedural, Program, and/or Equipment Requirements	Make available at the terminal a first aid kit appropriate for the hazards found in marine cargo handling operations. The kit's contents must be checked often enough to ensure prompt replacement of needed or expired items. Provide stretchers in operable condition for each vessel being worked. Provide a life ring at each waterside work area where there is potential for drowning. Provide a telephone or other effective means of communication.
Training Requirements	When work is in progress, at least one person must have a current first aid certificate to provide first aid care.
Assistance Tools	Standard – 29 CFR 1917.26 *First aid and lifesaving facilities.*

4.   29 CFR 1917.30 *Emergency action plans*

An emergency action plan establishes procedures that prevent fatalities, injuries, and property damage. The plan must cover the actions the employer and employees are to take to ensure employee safety in the case of fire or other emergencies.

Procedural, Program, and/or Equipment Requirements	Prepare an emergency action plan. The plan does not need to be written and may be communicated orally if there are 10 or fewer employees. At a minimum, the plan must include • Escape procedures and escape routes, • Procedures for those who remain to conduct critical operations prior to evacuation, • Procedures to account for employees after evacuation, • The rescue and medical duties of employees, • The fire and emergency reporting procedures, and • Who to contact for further information or explanation about the plan. Establish an emergency alarm system for emergency action and/or evacuation. If employees are directed to respond to an emergency that is beyond the scope of the emergency action plan required by 29 CFR 1917.30, then ensure compliance with the requirements of 29 CFR 1910.120(q).

Training Requirements	Review the emergency action plan with each employee when the plan is developed, when they are initially assigned to work, his or her responsibilities change or the plan changes.
	Train employee(s) who are expected to assist in the safe and orderly evacuation.
Assistance Tools	Standard – 29 CFR 1917.30 *Emergency action plans.*

5. **29 CFR 1917.128** *Signs and marking*

This standard for terminal facilities includes requirements for posting of signs for first aid facilities, firefighting and emergency equipment, exits, and emergency contact information.

Procedural, Program, and/or Equipment Requirements	Conspicuously post signs for locations of first aid facilities, telephones, firefighting and emergency equipment, and fire exits.
	Conspicuously post telephone numbers of the closest ambulance service, hospital or other source of medical attention, police, fire department, and emergency squad (if any).
Assistance Tools	Standard – 29 CFR 1917.128 *Signs and marking.*

B. Additional Requirements for Workplaces Referenced in Other Requirements

There are no additional requirements for workplaces referenced in other requirements.

C. Additional Requirements for Specific Workplaces/Operations

1. **29 CFR 1917.1** *Scope and applicability* **(29 CFR 1910 Subpart T** *Commercial Diving applies to marine terminals)*

See Section I.C.15. (29 CFR 1910 Subpart T).

2. **29 CFR 1917.73** *Termination facilities handling menhaden and similar species of fish*

This standard addresses termination facilities handling menhaden and similar species of fish. It includes requirements for personal protective and rescue equipment for hazardous atmospheres, stand-by rescue personnel for entry into hazardous atmospheres, and employee training.

Training Requirements	Appropriately train the plant superintendent and foremen about the hazards of hydrogen sulfide and oxygen deficiency, the use of appropriate respiratory and other protective equipment, and the rescue procedures. Inform other supervisory plant personnel of hydrogen sulfide and oxygen deficiency hazards and instruct them in the necessary safety measures, including use of respiratory and rescue equipment.
Assistance Tools	Standard – 29 CFR 1917.73 *Termination facilities handling menhaden and similar species of fish.*

D. Requirements that Support Emergency Response and Preparedness

1. 29 CFR 1917.25 *Fumigants, pesticides, insecticides, and hazardous preservatives*

This standard covers fumigants, pesticides, insecticides, and hazardous preservatives at marine terminal operations. The standard includes requirements for providing emergency protective equipment and training employees who enter spaces containing hazardous atmospheres.

Procedural, Program, and/or Equipment Requirements	Allow only designated persons to enter hazardous atmospheres. Provide and ensure the use of appropriate respiratory and emergency protective equipment for persons entering a space containing a hazardous atmosphere. Similarly equip standby observers.
Training Requirements	Provide instruction to persons entering a space containing a hazardous atmosphere on the nature of the hazard(s), precautions to be taken, and the use of protective and emergency equipment. Ensure standby observers continuously monitor the activity of employees within spaces containing a hazardous atmosphere.
Assistance Tools	Standard – 29 CFR 1917.25 *Fumigants, pesticides, insecticides and hazardous preservatives.*

2.　29 CFR 1917.28 *Hazard communication*

See Section I.D.5. (29 CFR 1910.1200).

3.　29 CFR 1917.92 *Respiratory protection*

See Section I.D.2. (29 CFR 1910.134).

4.　29 CFR 1917.95 *Other protective measures*

This marine terminal standard includes requirements for protective clothing, personal flotation devices, and emergency facilities.

Procedural, Program, and/or Equipment Requirements	When employees are exposed to hazardous substances that may require emergency bathing, eye-washing, or other facilities, provide and maintain such facilities.
Assistance Tools	Standard – 29 CFR 1917.95 *Other protective measures*.

NOTE: In addition to the marine terminal standards highlighted in this publication, the following standards also contain limited emergency-related requirements: 29 CFR 1917.45 Cranes and derricks; 1917.49 Spouts, chutes, hoppers, bins, and associated equipment; 1917.117 Manlifts; and 1917.157 Battery charging and changing.

IV. Longshoring (29 CFR 1918) Requirements for Emergency Response and Preparedness

A. General Requirements for Workplaces

1. 29 CFR 1918.93 *Hazardous atmospheres and substances*

This standard covers areas where the employer knows, or has reason to believe, that a hazardous atmosphere or substance may exist. Requirements cover hazard determination, testing during ventilation, and entry into areas containing hazardous atmospheres.

Procedural, Program, and/or Equipment Requirements	Protect persons entering a space containing a hazardous atmosphere by providing appropriate respiratory and emergency protective equipment. Standby observers must continuously monitor the activities of employees who enter an area containing a hazardous atmosphere.
Training Requirements	Provide instruction to persons entering a space containing a hazardous atmosphere regarding the hazards, precautions to be taken, and the use of protective and emergency equipment. Standby observers must also be instructed similarly. In emergency or rescue operations where entry into flammable or oxygen-deficient atmospheres is necessary, train employees as to the hazards and the use of SCBAs.
Assistance Tools	Standard – 29 CFR 1918.93 *Hazardous atmospheres and substances*.

2. 29 CFR 1918.94 *Ventilation and atmospheric conditions*

This standard covers ventilation and atmospheric conditions for the longshoring industry. It includes requirements concerning carbon monoxide, fumigated cargo, grain dust, and fish catches.

Procedural, Program, and/or Equipment Requirements	When employees are entering a compartment containing a hazardous or unknown concentration of fumigants for testing of the atmosphere, or for emergency purposes, protect each employee with appropriate respiratory protective equipment meeting the provisions of 29 CFR 1910.134 (per 29 CFR 1918.102).
	Provide any protective clothing and other PPE recommended by the fumigant manufacturer for protection against hazards.
	Ensure that at least two similarly equipped employees are stationed outside the compartment as observers, to provide rescue services in case of emergency.
	Provide one or more employees on duty to provide any specific emergency medical treatment stipulated for the particular fumigant.
	Ensure that emergency equipment is readily accessible wherever fumigated grains are being handled.

Training Requirements	Train employees who are to provide emergency care on any specific emergency medical treatment stipulated for the particular fumigant(s).
Assistance Tools	Standard – 29 CFR 1918.94 *Ventilation and atmospheric conditions.*

3. 29 CFR 1918.97 *First aid and lifesaving facilities*

This standard includes the requirements for first aid, stretchers, life-rings, and communication for the longshoring industry.

Procedural, Program, and/or Equipment Requirements	Make available at or near each vessel being worked a first aid kit appropriate for the hazards found in marine cargo handling facilities. The kit's contents must be checked often enough to ensure prompt replacement of needed or expired items.
	Provide stretchers in operable condition for each vessel being worked.
	Provide a life-ring and line in the vicinity for each vessel being worked and for each floating vessel.
	Provide a telephone or other effective means of communication.
Training Requirements	When work is in progress, ensure that at least one person has a current first aid certificate to render first aid.
Assistance Tools	Standard – 29 CFR 1918.97 *First aid and lifesaving facilities.*
	Standard Appendix – 29 CFR 1918 Appendix V, *Basic Elements of a First Aid Training Program (Non-mandatory).*

4. 29 CFR 1918.100 *Emergency action plans*

An emergency action plan establishes procedures that prevent fatalities, injuries, and property damage. The plan must cover the actions the employer and employees are to take to ensure employee safety in the case of fire or other emergencies.

Procedural, Program, and/or Equipment Requirements	Prepare an emergency action plan. The plan does not need to be written and may be communicated orally if there are 10 or fewer employees. At a minimum, the plan must include
	• Escape procedures and escape routes,
	• Procedures for those who remain to conduct critical operations prior to evacuation,
	• Procedures to account for employees after evacuation,
	• The rescue and medical duties of employees,
	• The fire and emergency reporting procedures, and
	• Who to contact for further information or explanation about the plan.

Procedural, Program, and/or Equipment Requirements (Continued)	Establish an emergency alarm system for emergency action and/or evacuation.
Training Requirements	Review the emergency action plan with each employee when the plan is developed, when they are initially assigned to work, his or her responsibilities change or the plan changes. Train employee(s) who are expected to assist in the safe and orderly evacuation.
Assistance Tools	Standard – 29 CFR 1918.100 *Emergency action plans.*

B. Additional Requirements for Workplaces Referenced in Other Requirements

There are no additional requirements for workplaces referenced in other requirements.

C. Additional Requirements for Specific Workplaces/Operations

1.　**29 CFR 1918.1** *Scope and application (29 CFR 1910 Subpart T Commercial Diving applies to marine terminals)*

See Section I.C.15. (29 CFR 1910 Subpart T).

D. Requirements that Support Emergency Response and Preparedness

1.　**29 CFR 1918.90** *Hazard communication*

See Section I.D.5. (29 CFR 1910.1200).

2.　**29 CFR 1918.102** *Respiratory protection*

See Section I.D.2. (29 CFR 1910.134).

NOTE: In addition to the longshoring standards highlighted in this publication, the following standards also contain limited emergency-related requirements: 29 CFR 1918.85 Containerized cargo operations; and 1918.88 Log operations.

V. Construction (29 CFR 1926) Requirements for Emergency Response and Preparedness

A. General Requirements for Workplaces

1. 29 CFR 1926.23 *First aid and medical attention, and* 1926.50 *Medical services and first aid*

These first aid and medical service requirements apply to construction work only. The standard establishes requirements for first aid and medical care for job-related injuries.

Procedural, Program, and/or Equipment Requirements	Make arrangements before a project begins to ensure that medical personnel are available for advice and consultation on occupational health matters.
	First aid supplies shall be easily accessible when required. Ensure that kits are checked before being sent out to a job and at least weekly to replace used items.
	Provide suitable facilities for immediate emergency use for quick drenching and flushing of the eyes and body, if exposure to corrosive materials is possible.
	Provide proper equipment to transport the injured person to a physician or hospital or a communication system for contacting necessary ambulance service.
	Post the telephone numbers of physicians, hospitals, or ambulances, where 911 service is not available.
Training Requirements	In the absence of readily accessible medical services, a person who has a valid certificate in first aid training from the U.S. Bureau of Mines, the American Red Cross, or equivalent training that can be verified by documentary evidence must be available at the worksite to render first aid.
Assistance Tools	Standard – 29 CFR 1926.23 *First aid and medical attention.*
	Standard – 29 CFR 1926.50 *Medical services and first aid.*
	Interpretation Letter – December 1, 1976, Ms. Deborah A. Moser, *Accessibility of a hospital or physician in terms of distance and travel time.*

2. 29 CFR 1926.24 *Fire protection and prevention,* 1926.150 *Fire protection, and* 1926.151 *Fire prevention*

These standards apply to construction, repair, alteration, and demolition work. The standards require the development of a fire prevention and protection program and the availability of fire suppression equipment.

Procedural, Program, and/or Equipment Requirements	Develop a fire protection program to provide equipment for potential fire hazards. Conspicuously locate firefighting equipment.
	Provide fire extinguishers and other firefighting equipment based on site conditions and site fire hazards (fire classes).
	Periodically inspect and maintain firefighting equipment. Replace defective equipment.
	Where warranted by the project, provide a trained and equipped firefighting organization (fire brigade).
	Establish an alarm system to alert employees on the site and the local fire department of an emergency. Post alarm code(s) and reporting instructions at phones and at employee entrances.
	Ensure that material storage and potential ignition sources do not create a fire hazard. Store materials so that exits are not impeded.
Training Requirements	If a fire brigade is necessary, adequately train the fire brigade.
Assistance Tools	Standard – 29 CFR 1926.24 *Fire protection and prevention*.
	Standard – 29 CFR 1926.150 *Fire protection*.
	Standard – 29 CFR 1926.151 *Fire prevention*.

3. 29 CFR 1926.34 *Means of egress*

This standard provides requirements to ensure that egress is unobstructed and clearly marked.

Procedural, Program, and/or Equipment Requirements	Maintain unobstructed egress from every building and structure where employees are working.
	Mark all exits with signs and mark access to exits where it is not immediately apparent how to exit.
Assistance Tools	Standard – 29 CFR 1926.34 *Means of egress*.

B. Additional Requirements for Workplaces Referenced in Other Requirements

1. 29 CFR 1926.35 *Employee emergency action plans*

In preparing for fire and other emergencies, an emergency action plan establishes procedures to ensure employee safety and health. An emergency action plan is a workplace requirement when another applicable standard requires it. The following standards reference or require compliance with 1926.35: 29 CFR 1926.64 and 1926.65.

Procedural, Program, and/or Equipment Requirements	Prepare and implement a written emergency action plan. The plan does not need to be written and may be communicated orally if there are 10 or fewer employees. Develop a plan that includes • Emergency escape procedures and route assignment, • Procedures for those who remain to conduct critical operations, • Procedures to account for employees after the emergency, • Rescue and medical duties of those assigned to them, • Means of reporting fires and emergencies, and • Names or titles of those to contact for further information about the plan. Establish an employee alarm system.
Training Requirements	Review the emergency action plan with each employee when the plan is developed, responsibilities shift, or the emergency procedures change. Provide specific training to employees who are expected to assist in the evacuation.
Assistance Tools	Standard – 29 CFR 1926.35 *Employee emergency action plans*.

C. Additional Requirements for Specific Workplaces/Operations

1. CFR 29 1926.60 *Methylenedianiline*

This section covers occupational exposures to Methylenedianiline (MDA) in construction work, except as provided by the standard. The standard requires a written plan for emergencies and addresses emergency alerting means and escape, protective equipment, and medical surveillance. "Emergency" means any occurrence such as, but not limited to, equipment failure, rupture of containers, or failure of control equipment that results in an unexpected and potentially hazardous release of MDA.

Procedural, Program, and/or Equipment Requirements	Develop and implement a written plan for emergency situations where there is a possibility of an emergency. At a minimum, the plan must • Identify emergency escape routes for employees at each construction site before the construction operation begins. • Specifically provide that employees engaged in correcting emergency conditions shall be equipped with the appropriate PPE and clothing until the emergency is abated. • Include elements prescribed in Emergency action plans (29 CFR 1910.38) and Fire prevention plans (29 CFR 1910.39). Where there is the possibility of employee exposure to MDA due to an emergency, provide means to promptly alert employees who have the potential to be directly exposed. Ensure that employees not engaged in correcting emergency conditions are immediately evacuated in the event of an emergency. Select and provide <u>appropriate</u> respirators for use during emergencies. Make available a medical surveillance program, as provided by the standard, for employees exposed to MDA during an emergency situation.
Training Requirements	Provide employees with information and training on MDA, in accordance with 29 CFR 1910.1200 (h), at the time of initial assignment and at least annually thereafter. Ensure that employees who must wear respiratory protection, including those who do not evacuate but stay to handle emergencies, receive training consistent with 29 CFR 1910.134.
Assistance Tools	Standard – 29 CFR 1926.60 *Methylenedianiline.* Standard Appendix – 1926.60 Appendix A, *Substance data sheet,* for 4,4'-Methylenedianiline.

2. CFR 29 1926.64 *Process safety management (PSM) of highly hazardous chemicals*

See Section I.C.3. (29 CFR 1910.119)

3. 29 CFR 1926.65 *Hazardous waste operations and emergency response, paragraphs (b) Safety and health program through (o) New technology programs*

See Section I.C.4. (29 CFR 1910.120, paragraphs (b)-(o)).

4.   29 CFR 1926.65, paragraph (p) *Certain operations conducted under the Resource Conservation and Recovery Act of 1976 (RCRA)*

See Section I.C.5. (29 CFR 1910.120, paragraph (p))

5.   29 CFR 1926.65, paragraph (q) *Emergency response to hazardous substance releases*

See Section I.C.6. (29 CFR 1910.120, paragraph (q))

6.   29 CFR 1926.651 *Specific excavation requirements*

This standard provides safety and rescue requirements for work in open excavations, including trenches.

Procedural, Program, and/or Equipment Requirements	Provide emergency rescue equipment, such as a respirator, a safety harness and lifeline, or a basket stretcher when an excavation contains or potentially contains a hazardous atmosphere. Ensure that person(s) attend the equipment in case of emergency.
	Provide and ensure the use of a safety harness and lifeline when employee(s) perform work in bell-bottom pier holes, or other similar deep and confined footing excavations. Ensure that person(s) attend the lifeline while worker(s) are in the excavation.
Assistance Tools	Standard – 29 CFR 1926.651 *Specific excavation requirements.*

7.   29 CFR 1926.800 *Underground construction*

This section applies to the construction of underground tunnels, shafts, chambers, and passageways. This section also applies to cut-and-cover excavations which are both physically connected to ongoing underground construction operations within the scope of this section, and covered in such a manner as to create conditions characteristic of underground construction. It includes emergency provisions for evacuation and employee check-in/check-out.

Procedural, Program, and/or Equipment Requirements	Where there is a potential environmental or structural failure hazard, develop and maintain a check-in/check-out procedure to provide an accurate count of the number of persons underground in the event of an emergency.
	For work in underground hazardous locations, provide means to summon emergency assistance to an employee working alone who is not being observed or can't request assistance by voice.
	Ensure hoist shafts used as means of egress during emergency include power-assisted

Procedural, Program, and/or Equipment Requirements (Continued)	hoisting capability, unless the regular hoisting means can operate during electrical power failure. Ensure that air monitoring is performed meeting the requirements of 29 CFR 1926.800(j). When continuous sampling indicates that hydrogen sulfide concentrations reach 20 parts per million, a visual and aural alarm shall signal additional measures, such as respirator use, increased ventilation, or employee evacuation. Whenever 20 percent or more of the lower explosive limit for methane or other flammable gases is detected, employees, except those necessary to eliminate the hazard, shall be immediately evacuated to a safe location above ground. Select, provide, and make immediately available NIOSH approved self-rescuers to all employees in underground areas where employees might be trapped by smoke or gas. Designate at least one person to be on duty above ground to summon emergency aid for, and keep count of, underground employees. Provide an acceptable portable hand lamp or cap lamp to each underground employee for emergency use, unless natural light or an emergency lighting system is sufficient for escape. Establish at least two 5-person rescue teams for jobsites where 25 or more employees work underground at one time. Establish at least one rescue team where there are less than 25 employees working underground. Ensure that underground construction operations meet the fire prevention and control requirements provided by 29 CFR 1926.800(m).
Training Requirements	Instruct all employees on fire prevention and protection and emergency procedures, including evacuation plans and check-in/check-out systems. Qualify, at least annually, rescue team members in rescue procedures, the use and limitations of respirators, and the use of firefighting equipment. On sites where hazardous levels of flammable or noxious gases are found or anticipated, ensure that rescue team members practice monthly the donning and use of SCBAs. Ensure that rescue teams are familiar with jobsite conditions.
Assistance Tools	Standard – 29 CFR 1926.800 *Underground construction.* Interpretation Letter – May 3, 2001, Mr. Craig Jorsch, *Application of 1926.800 to lone employees working underground in a tunnel or shaft connected to a tunnel.*

8.   29 CFR 1926.950 *General requirements (Power Transmission and Distribution)*

This standard covers erection of new electric transmission and distribution lines and equipment, and the alteration, conversion, and improvement of existing electric transmission and distribution lines and equipment. The standard includes specific emergency procedures and first aid requirements.

Procedural, Program, and/or Equipment Requirements	Provide spotlights or portable lights for emergency lighting when needed to work safely at night.
Training Requirements	Provide training and ensure that employees understand emergency procedures and first aid fundamentals including CPR. (Alternatively, meet the requirements of 29 CFR 1926.50(c), Note: See Section V.A.1.)
Assistance Tools	Standard – 29 CFR 1926.950 *General requirements (Power Transmission and Distribution).*

The following construction standards are identical to those set forth in the corresponding general industry standards (29 CFR Part 1910).

9.   **29 CFR 1926 Subpart T** *Diving Operations*
(29 CFR 1926.1071 Scope and application,
1926.1076 Qualifications of dive team,
1926.1080 Safe practice manual,
1926.1081 Pre-dive procedures, and
1926.1082 Procedures during dive)

See Section I.C.15. (29 CFR 1910 Subpart T)

10.   **29 CFR 1926.1103** *13 Carcinogens, etc. (4-Nitrobiphenyl, etc.);*
1926.1104 alpha-Naphthylamine,
1926.1106 Methyl chloromethyl ether,
1926.1107 3, 3'-Dichlorobenzidine (and its salts),
1926.1108 bis-Chloromethyl ether,
1926.1109 beta-Naphthylamine,
1926.1110 Benzidine,
1926.1111 4-Aminodiphenyl,
1926.1112 Ethyleneimine,
1926.1113 beta-Propiolactone,
1926.1114 2-Acetylaminofluorene,
1926.1115 4-Dimethylaminoazobenzene, and/or
1926.1116 N-Nitrosodimethylamine

See Section I.C.15. (29 CFR 1910.1003)

11.   **29 CFR 1926.1117** *Vinyl chloride*

See Section I.C.17. (29 CFR 1910.1017)

12.   29 CFR 1926.1127 *Cadmium*

This standard applies to all construction industry occupational exposures to cadmium and cadmium compounds, in all forms. The standard requires the development of a written plan for emergencies involving substantial releases of airborne cadmium and includes requirements for employee training on emergencies and medical examinations.

Procedural, Program, and/or Equipment Requirements	Develop and implement a written plan for dealing with emergency situations involving substantial releases of airborne cadmium. At a minimum, the plan must include • Provisions for the use of appropriate respirators and personal protective equipment; and • Restrictions for employees not essential to correcting the emergency situation from the area and normal operations halted in that area until the emergency is abated. Select and provide appropriate respirators for emergencies. Provide required medical examinations as soon as possible to any employee who may have been acutely exposed to cadmium because of an emergency.
Training Requirements	Provide training, including training on emergency procedures, prior to or at the time of initial assignment to a job involving potential exposure to cadmium and at least annually thereafter. Ensure that employees who must wear respiratory protection, including those who do not evacuate but stay to handle emergencies, receive training consistent with 29 CFR 1910.134.
Assistance Tools	Standard – 29 CFR 1926.1127 *Cadmium.* Standard Appendix – 1926.1127 Appendix A, *Substance Safety Data Sheet – Cadmium.*

13.   29 CFR 1926.1128 *Benzene*

See Section I.C.19. (29 CFR 1910.1028)

14.   29 CFR 1926.1129 *Coke oven emissions*

Note: See Section I.C.20. (29 CFR 1910.1029)

15.   29 CFR 1926.1144 *1,2-dibromo-3-chloropropane*

See Section I.C.21. (29 CFR 1910.1044)

16.   29 CFR 1926.1145 *Acrylonitrile*

See Section I.C.22. (29 CFR 1910.1045)

17.   29 CFR 1926.1147 *Ethylene oxide*

See Section I.C.23. (29 CFR 1910.1047)

18.   29 CFR 1926.1148 *Formaldehyde*

See Section I.C.24. (29 CFR 1910.1048)

19.   29 CFR 1926.1152 *Methylene Chloride*

See Section I.C.27. (29 CFR 1910.1052)

D. Requirements that Support Emergency Response and Preparedness

1.   29 CFR 1926.28 *Personal protective equipment* and 1926.95 *Criteria for personal protective equipment*

These general PPE standards address the availability and use of protective equipment for employees. The standard requires that appropriate equipment be chosen based on site conditions and hazards and that the employer ensure the equipment's use.

Procedural, Program, and/or Equipment Requirements	Provide and ensure the use and maintenance of appropriate PPE for site operations and hazards. Ensure any employee-owned equipment is adequate and properly maintained.
Assistance Tools	Standard – 29 CFR 1926.28 *Personal protective equipment.* Standard – 29 CFR 1926.95 *Criteria for personal protective equipment.*

2. 29 CFR 1926.55 *Gases, vapors, fumes, dusts, and mists*

This standard establishes employee exposure limits for air contaminants. The standard includes ceiling limits and 8-hour time-weighted average limits for contaminants.

Procedural, Program, and/or Equipment Requirements	Ensure that employee exposures do not exceed the limits provided by the standard. Exposures should be limited through engineering controls, administrative controls, and, as a last resort, PPE.
Assistance Tools	Standard – 29 CFR 1926.55 *Gases, vapors, fumes, dusts, and mists.* Standard Appendix – 1926.55 Appendix A, *Gases, vapors, fumes, dusts, and mists.*

3. 29 CFR 1926.59 *Hazard communication*

See Section I.D.5. (29 CFR 1910.1200)

4. 29 CFR 1926.103 *Respiratory protection*

See Section I.D.2. (29 CFR 1910.134)

NOTE: In addition to the construction standards highlighted in this publication, the following standards also contain limited emergency related requirements: 29 CFR1926.803 Compressed air; 1926.955 Overhead lines; and 1926.956 Underground lines.

VI. Agriculture (29 CFR 1928) Requirements for Emergency Response and Preparedness

A. General Requirements for Workplaces

1.   29 CFR 1928.21 *Applicability of Standards in 29 CFR Part 1910*

This standard provides that certain standards contained in 29 CFR 1910 (General Industry) are applicable to agricultural operations. Several of the standards, listed below, contain emergency-related requirements.

- Logging operations, 29 CFR 1910.266 (See Section I.C.11.)

- Storage and handling of anhydrous ammonia, 29 CFR 1910.111(a) and (b) (See Section I.C.2.)

- Hazard communication, 29 CFR 1910.1200 (See Section I.D.5.)

- Cadmium, 29 CFR 1910.1027 (See Section I.C.18.)

Additional Online Emergency Assistance Information

OSHA

OSHA's Emergency Preparedness and Response Page

This webpage provides links to Emergency Preparedness and Response materials to assist employers and employees in planning for all types of emergencies in the workplace. Guidance published includes the *Evacuation Planning Matrix, Evacuation eTool,* and the *Fire and Explosion Matrix.* The webpage also includes a link to OSHA's electronic Health and Safety Plan (e-HASP). The electronic, interactive e-HASP Guide is intended to be used by health and safety professionals to provide "model" language in preparing a site's HASP.

How to Plan for Workplace Emergencies and Evacuations – OSHA Publication 3088

The booklet is written to help employers plan for emergencies and develop an emergency action plan.

Other Sources of Information

Department of Homeland Security Website

Federal Emergency Management Agency Website

National Response Team Website

State Emergency Response Agency Websites

DOT's 2002 Emergency Response Guidebook (ERG2002)

OSHA Assistance

OSHA provides assistance and guidance through a variety of programs and resources, including State Programs, workplace Consultation, Voluntary Protection Programs, Strategic Partnerships, Alliances, training, education and outreach, and more. An overall commitment to workplace safety and health can add value to your business, to your workplace, and to your life. We encourage employers to take advantage of these programs and resources.

State Programs

The *Occupational Safety and Health Act of 1970* (OSH Act) encourages states to develop and operate their own job safety and health plans. OSHA approves and monitors these plans. There are currently 26 state plans: 22 cover both private and public (state and local government) employment; state plans of 4 states, Connecticut, New Jersey, New York, and the Virgin Islands cover the public sector only. States and territories with their own OSHA-approved occupational safety and health plans must adopt standards identical to, or at least as effective as, the Federal standards, and therefore may have more stringent or supplemental requirements. Contact information for the OSHA-approved state plans is available on OSHA's website at www.osha.gov/oshdir/states.html.

Consultation Services

Consultation assistance is available on request to employers who want help in establishing and maintaining a safe and healthful workplace. Largely funded by OSHA, the service is provided at no cost to the employer. Primarily developed for smaller employers with more hazardous operations, the Consultation Service is delivered by state governments employing professional safety and health consultants. Comprehensive assistance includes an appraisal of all mechanical systems, work practices, and occupational safety and health hazards in the workplace and all aspects of the employer's present job safety and health program. In addition, the service offers assistance to employers in developing and implementing an effective safety and health program. No penalties are proposed or citations issued for hazards identified by the consultant if the employer abates the hazards in a timely manner. OSHA provides consultation assistance to the employer with the assurance that his or her name and firm and any information about the workplace will not be routinely reported to OSHA enforcement staff.

Under the consultation program, certain exemplary employers may request participation in OSHA's Safety and Health Achievement Recognition Program (SHARP). Eligibility for participation in SHARP includes receiving a comprehensive consultation visit, demonstrating exemplary achievements in workplace safety and health by abating all identified hazards, and developing an excellent safety and health program.

Employers accepted into SHARP may receive an exemption from programmed inspections (not complaint or accident investigation inspections) for a period of 1 year. For more information concerning consultation assistance, visit OSHA's website at www.osha.gov/dcsp/smallbusiness/consult.html.

Voluntary Protection Programs (VPP)

Voluntary Protection Programs and on-site consultation services, when coupled with an effective enforcement program, expand worker protection to help meet the goals of the OSH Act.

The three VPP – Star, Merit, and Demonstration – are designed to recognize outstanding achievements by companies that have successfully incorporated comprehensive safety and health programs into their total management system. The VPP motivates others to achieve excellent safety and health results in the same outstanding way as they establish a cooperative relationship between employers, employees, and OSHA.

For additional information on VPP and how to apply, contact the VPP managers in the OSHA regional offices listed at the end of this publication or consult the VPP information on the OSHA website at www.osha.gov/dcsp/vpp/index.html.

Strategic Partnership Program

OSHA's Strategic Partnership Program, the newest of OSHA's cooperative programs, helps encourage, assist and recognize the efforts of partners to eliminate serious workplace hazards and achieve a high level of worker safety and health. Whereas OSHA's Consultation Program and VPP entail one-on-one relationships between OSHA and individual worksites, most strategic partnerships seek to have a broader impact by building cooperative relationships with groups of employers and employees. These partnerships are voluntary, cooperative relationships between OSHA, employers, employee representatives and others (e.g., trade unions, trade and professional associations, universities and other government agencies).

For more information on this and other cooperative programs, contact your nearest OSHA office or visit OSHA's website at www.osha.gov/dcsp/compliance_assistance/index_programs.html.

Alliance Program

Alliances enable organizations committed to workplace safety and health to collaborate with OSHA to prevent injuries and illnesses in the workplace. OSHA and its allies work together to reach out to, educate and lead the nation's employers and their employees in improving and advancing workplace safety and health.

Alliances are open to all, including trade or professional organizations, businesses, labor organizations, educational institutions and government agencies. In some cases, organizations may be building on existing relationships with OSHA through other cooperative programs.

There are few formal program requirements for alliances, which are less structured than other cooperative agreements, and the agreements do not include an enforcement component. However, OSHA and the participating organizations must define, implement and meet a set of short- and long-term goals that fall into three categories: training and education; outreach and communication; and promotion of the national dialogue on workplace safety and health.

Training and Education

OSHA's area offices offer a variety of information services, such as compliance assistance, technical advice, publications, audiovisual aids and speakers for special engagements. OSHA's Training Institute in Arlington Heights, IL, provides basic and advanced courses in safety and health for Federal and state compliance officers, state consultants, Federal agency personnel and private sector employers, employees and their representatives.

The OSHA Training Institute also has established OSHA Training Institute Education Centers to address the increased demand for its courses from the private sector and from other Federal agencies. These centers are nonprofit colleges, universities and other organizations that have been selected after a competition for participation in the program.

OSHA also provides funds to nonprofit organizations, through grants, to conduct workplace training and education in subjects where OSHA believes there is a lack of workplace training.

Grants are awarded annually. Grant recipients are expected to contribute 20 percent of the total grant cost.

For more information on grants, training and education, contact the OSHA Training Institute, Office of Training and Education, 2020 S. Arlington Heights Road, Arlington Heights, IL 60005, (847) 297-4810. For further information on any OSHA program, contact your nearest OSHA area or regional office listed at the end of this publication.

Electronic Information

OSHA has a variety of materials and tools available on its website www.osha.gov. These include e-Tools such as Expert Advisors, Electronic Compliance Assistance Tools (e-cats), Technical Links; regulations, directives, publications, videos and other information for employers and employees. OSHA's software programs and compliance assistance tools walk you through challenging safety and health issues and common problems to find the best solutions for your workplace.

OSHA Publications

OSHA has an extensive publications program. For a listing of free or sales items, visit OSHA's website at www.osha.gov/pls/publications/pubindex.list or contact the OSHA Publications Office, U.S. Department of Labor, 200 Constitution Avenue, NW, N-3101, Washington, DC 20210. Telephone (202) 693-1888 or fax to (202) 693-2498.

Emergencies, Complaints or Further Assistance

To report an emergency, file a complaint, or seek OSHA advice, assistance, or products, call 1-800-321-OSHA or contact your nearest OSHA regional or area office. The teletypewriter (TTY) number is 1-877-889-5627.

You can also file a complaint online and obtain more information on OSHA Federal and state programs by visiting OSHA's website at www.osha.gov.

For more information on grants, training and education, contact the OSHA Training Institute, Office of Training and Education, 2020 S. Arlington Heights Road, Arlington Heights, IL 60005, (847) 297-4810, or see the Outreach Training Program on OSHA's website at www.osha.gov/fso/ote/training/outreach/training_program.html.

OSHA Regional Offices

Region I
(CT,* ME, MA, NH, RI, VT*)
JFK Federal Building, Room E340
Boston, MA 02203
(617) 565–9860

Region II
(NJ,* NY,* PR,* VI*)
201 Varick Street, Room 670
New York, NY 10014
(212) 337–2378

Region III
(DE, DC, MD,* PA, VA,* WV)
The Curtis Center
170 S. Independence Mall West
Suite 740 West
Philadelphia, PA 19106-3309
(215) 861–4900

Region IV
(AL, FL, GA, KY,* MS, NC,* SC,* TN*)
SNAF
61 Forsyth Street SW, Room 6T50
Atlanta, GA 30303
(404) 562–2300

Region V
(IL, IN,* MI,* MN,* OH, WI)
230 South Dearborn Street, Room 3244
Chicago, IL 60604
(312) 353–2220

Region VI
(AR, LA, NM,* OK, TX)
525 Griffin Street, Room 602
Dallas, TX 75202
(214) 767–4731 or 4736 x224

Region VII

(IA,* KS, MO, NE)
City Center Square
1100 Main Street, Suite 800
Kansas City, MO 64105
(816) 426–5861

Region VIII

(CO, MT, ND, SD, UT,* WY*)
1999 Broadway, Suite 1690
PO Box 46550
Denver, CO 80201-6550
(303) 844–1600

Region IX

(American Samoa, AZ,* CA,* HI,* NV,* Northern
Mariana Islands)
71 Stevenson Street, Room 420
San Francisco, CA 94105
(415) 975–4310

Region X

(AK,* ID, OR,* WA*)
1111 Third Avenue, Suite 715
Seattle, WA 98101-3212
(206) 553–5930

*These states and territories operate their own OSHA-approved job safety and health programs (Connecticut, New Jersey, New York and Puerto Rico plans cover public employees only). States with approved programs must have a standard that is identical to, or at least as effective as, the Federal standard.

Note: To get contact information for OSHA Area Offices, OSHA-approved State Plans, and OSHA Consultation Projects, please visit us online at www.osha.gov or call us at (800) 321-OSHA (6742).

www.osha.gov

OSHA's role is to assure the safety and health of America's workers by setting and enforcing standards; providing training, outreach and education; establishing partnerships; and encouraging continual improvement in workplace safety and health.

This informational booklet provides a general overview of a particular topic related to OSHA standards. It does not alter or determine compliance responsibilities in OSHA standards or the *Occupational Safety and Health Act of 1970.* Because interpretations and enforcement policy may change over time, you should consult current OSHA administrative interpretations, and decisions by the Occupational Safety and Health Review Commission and the Courts for additional guidance on OSHA compliance requirements.

This information is available to sensory impaired individuals upon request. Voice phone: (202) 693-1999; teletypewriter (TTY) number: (877) 889-5627.

**Occupational Safety
and Health Administration**

U.S. Department of Labor

www.osha.gov